D1257643

Thirty Years
with the
Big Bands

THIRTY YEARS
WITH THE
BIG BANDS

by

ARTHUR ROLLINI

UNIVERSITY OF ILLINOIS PRESS

Urbana and Chicago

First published in 1987 by
The Macmillan Press Ltd
London
England

Published in 1987 in the United States by
University of Illinois Press
Urbana and Chicago

Typeset by Rowland Phototypesetting Ltd
Bury St Edmunds, Suffolk
in 11/13pt Caledonia

Printed in Hong Kong

ISBN 0-252-01454-5

Contents

Foreword

This book is dedicated to my daughter Adrienne, named after her talented uncle Adrian, who was eight and a half years my senior and an inspiration to me to follow his footsteps in a musical career.

I wish to thank Barbara Gideon, Mary Fritchie and Elizabeth Buley for transcribing this book. Also, thanks to Dennis O'Brian and Ruth Goetz of the Middle Island Library for their research on certain material, plus George T. Simon and Leonard Feather for their support.

I hope my readers enjoy this true life story.

Musically Yours,
Art Rollini

ONE

A childhood in Larchmont

I was born Arthur Francis Rollini on 13 February 1912. My birthday was sandwiched between those of two great men: Abraham Lincoln on February 12th, and St Valentine, who lived in the third century, on February 14th. I do not claim to be even one percent as phenomenal as these two great Aquarius men, but believe that I am one hundred percent their equal in loving everyone, hating no one and fearing no one but God.

My father was the son of Antoine Rollins (pronounced Rollan), a French general who was defeated in the Franco-Prussian War of 1870–71. He then made his escape to Italy, dropped the "s" from the end of his name, inserted an "i" and became Antonio Rollini. Italy had been in sympathy with France and greeted him cordially. A title of Baron was bestowed upon him and he married an Italian girl. My dad was the eldest of three children, with two girls following, my Aunts Giga and Julia.

On my mother's side, there were Michel and Maria Augenti, who had six children: Adelina (Adele), Francesco (whose name I inherited as a middle name), Rosa (Rose), Lillian and Mildred. One other child died at an early age. All of them were musically inclined. My Uncle Francesco later cut his name to Frank, although some of his wives called him Francis. I say "some of his wives" in earnest. This man died in 1980 at the age of ninety-nine. He outlived three wives, and, at the age of ninety-six, married a fourth, Maria, who was just a little more than half his age. At that time Uncle Francis (Frank) still played piano beautifully; he taped programs from TV and radio and sent them to his friends all over the country. He was fully aware of what was going on, was an avid Mets baseball fan, and was interested in photography, both still and motion. He was also interested in astronomy and astrology. His father, Michel, died in 1939 at the age of eighty-nine.

I was not an unwanted child, merely unplanned. My father, Baron Ferdinando Rollini, was chief artist and engraver for the American Tobacco Company. We lived in a brownstone house in Long Island City, New York, within view of the great Queensboro Bridge, which links the borough of Queens to the borough of Manhattan. My Aunt Lillian, on my mother's side, won a poll conducted by the *New York Journal* and became the "Queen" of the Queensboro Bridge. When the bridge was completed in 1909 she was the first woman to cross it and she cut the tape with Mayor William J. Gaynor. The retinue, or cortege, followed, led by Uncle Frank in his new car.

My first memory of anything at all was in the summer of 1915, when my family, including Mother, Dad, my brother Adrian, my sister Elvira, and I, moved into a summer home in Atlantic Highlands, New Jersey. Adrian was eight and a half years my senior (born 28 June 1903), and Elvira was four years and three months older than I (born 7 November 1907). We had a sandbox in our yard next to the house. I was playing there one day with my so-called friend, and the brat threw sand in my eyes and mouth. That startled me to the beginning of life. I screamed vehemently and my mother, Adelina (Adele), came running out of the house. She gently cleaned my eyes and mouth and gave the boy a good scolding.

The next thing I remember, after returning to Long Island City in September, was viewing the brass and crystal Ansonia clock on our mantel. This clock was a miniature which gonged softly on the hour and on the half hour. This little clock, which I later found out was manufactured in 1880, never ceased functioning as long as it was wound every eighth day. It was always wound on time and its little mercury pendulum kept beating back and forth and intrigued me. I would view it for hours.

In September 1916, when I was four and a half years old, I was sent to kindergarten. This was short-lived, however, because after two weeks, and being too shy to ask the teacher for permission to go to the toilet, I defecated in my pants. I was immediately expelled from school, to my chagrin. The teacher contacted my parents and told them that I was too young. My parents tried again in January 1917, when I was not quite five years old. This time I was successful, completing the grade in June. I had it made.

During this time my dad, the Baron, was very busy with plans of a beautiful home that he was building in Larchmont, New York. He was being assisted by a builder by the name of Santora, and an architect, Henry Cipolla. I started first grade in September 1917 and was doing fine, when on October 4th we moved to Larchmont. I was amazed at this comfortable home. It was of Spanish style with a red tile roof, stone fireplace, white stucco exterior and huge brick terrace. It had another building in back—chauffeur's quarters. My dad had bought property from Summit Avenue to Concord Avenue, a whole block away.

The main house consisted of five bedrooms, two and a half bathrooms and a john in the basement in the laundry room. We had a huge living room with a stone fireplace, a dining room, sun porch, and a huge kitchen with a pantry which was later converted to a breakfast nook. There was also an office in the attic for Dad. The chauffeur's quarters consisted of, of course, a two-car garage, plus a living room, two bedrooms, bath, dining room, kitchen and basement, all of which was styled like the main house.

When Dad did not feel like taking the 8:13 a.m. train to his office in New York City he would work tirelessly in his office at home for hours on end, peering through three magnifying glasses. My mother would take lunch up to him and he would take a short breather and then go back to work. We would not see him until the evening.

Adrian by now was an accomplished musician. For Christmas 1905 Santa Claus had given him a toy piano. He was about two and a half years old then. He was soon picking out melodies and playing the harmony parts. Often, half an hour after leaving his little piano, he would sing the songs in the same key as he had played them. My father, being a fine musician himself, soon detected this. Dad sang beautifully in church and also played piano and classical guitar superbly. He often hobnobbed with Caruso, Scotti, Galli-Curci, and Gigli of the Met. He was a beautiful singer, no doubt, but he lacked the power to be an opera singer. Nevertheless, he knew most of the operas, lyrics and music, by heart.

Adrian had absolute pitch. My father contacted Madame Negri, a fine piano teacher in New York City, and young Adrian started to take piano lessons at the tender age of three and a half. My dad had raised pedals installed on the piano and little Adrian went to work. Madame Negri visited weekly and Adrian progressed above the wildest imagination. When Adrian was four and a half years old, Madame Negri arranged for a fifteen-minute recital at the Waldorf Astoria Hotel in New York. Adrian went on stage, raised foot pedals and all, and played Chopin's *Minute Waltz* flawlessly. This was followed by more intricate pieces. At the end of the recital Adrian was besieged by the New York press and they proclaimed him a child prodigy. He went on to study with Madame Negri for a total of eleven years.

At Larchmont we had a brand new 1917 Model-T Ford and chauffeur's quarters, but we had no chauffeur! My mother and dad did not drive. They were both too nervous to do so and found the Model-T much too intricate. My mother tried it once, backing out of our driveway. She was doing well until she reached the road, Summit Avenue. A sewer line was under construction on our street, and the Sicilian laborers had been blasting this solid rock for months. Two planks were placed over the ditch for access in and out of our driveway. My mother backed directly into the ditch, however, missing the planks entirely. She gave up! We had the car hauled out and Adrian piped up, "Don't worry Mom, I'll drive you."

Mother said, "Adrian, you are too young."

Adrian replied, "I'll take care of it." That he did. He got a heavy pillow and placed it on the driver's seat, put an unlighted American Tobacco Company cigarette in his mouth, a cap on his head, and drove Mother and Dad everywhere. He made friends with all the police, including tough motorcycle officer Coughran, and would invite them to our home for cigarettes, of which my dad had an abundance from work. Dad did not smoke cigarettes, just an occasional cigar. The police would besiege our home for cigarettes and Adrian would entertain them with his magnificent piano playing. Adrian could do no wrong. He had carte blanche in the village of Larchmont, Westchester County, New York. He would often ask for the family car to visit his girlfriend, Rose Donah, at night. Mother and Dad let him have it, and he would come home at the hour requested. He was only fourteen years old.

Adrian had formed a band in grade school and high school. Mr Conklin, the wonderful music teacher at both Chatsworth Avenue Grade School and Mamaroneck High School, marveled at him. Adrian had such a keen ear that, when we were walking down the street and heard a trolley car squeal rounding a curve, he would shout excitedly, "A♭, kid!" He always called me "kid" until the day he died in 1956.

When I was eight years old Adrian bought me a snare drum, stand, and a couple pairs of drum sticks. He taught me to accompany his piano playing. He would give me the opportunity to play all of the fill-ins and breaks. We would play together for hours. Shortly after that Adrian went out on his own.

Things were going well for me in grade school. I was getting straight A's, well up in the nineties. In the third grade, Mr Conklin, our music teacher, handed song-books to us and they were in two-part harmony. I soon learned to read music and always sang the harmony parts. With his pitch-pipe he would give us the key, and we were off on our merry way. Mr Conklin had a beautiful tenor voice and played piano well. He was to follow me through grade school and high school.

In June 1925 I was graduated from grade school with high honors and vowed to take the tough college entrance course in Bachelor of Arts and eventually go to Columbia University. Adrian had quit high school after his second year. He said to Dad, "I have bigger things to do." He did just that. At the age of sixteen he went to New York City and negotiated a contract with Republic piano rolls. These rolls were far ahead of their time and stand up to this day. He recorded some twenty rolls.

Meanwhile my dad had purchased a summer home in upstate New York, in Clinton Hollow, Dutchess County. We went there the summer after I was graduated. It was on a hill overlooking a deep valley with a stream running along the bottom, and there was another hill on the other side. We would see cars on the other side, looking like little toys. It was truly a magnificent sight. During the daytime I would fish, catching pickerel, perch, bass, catfish, and large sunfish, and I would always have a good catch for dinner. We had rented both town houses for the summer and we were content. Dad had set up an office and mailed his work to New York.

In 1925 Adrian succeeded Arthur Hand as leader of the California Ramblers owing to Hand's retirement on account of illness. This was a top swing band in its day, playing at the California Ramblers' Inn near the Bronx–Westchester County border, near Pelham. Adrian had mastered the bass sax in a matter of weeks, and recorded several hundred sides with this band for Perfect, Okeh, Edison, Golden Gate, Brunswick and Gennett records. He had also made many small-group recordings under the names of Little Ramblers, Varsity Eight, University Six, Birmingham Babies and Goofus Five.

Adrian lived with us at home in Larchmont and had a souped up Model-T Ford with a special racing body, which at that time could outrun almost any car on the road. Paul Whiteman, who owned an estate in Pelham, was a frequent visitor to the Ramblers' Inn. One Saturday night in 1925, Whiteman, after having quite a few drinks while listening to the band, stayed until closing time and walked out to Adrian's car with him. Upon seeing the car Whiteman, who was a car buff, said to Adrian, "I'll give you $700 for it." Adrian, who was "feeling no pain," accepted the offer. Whiteman promptly pulled out his check-book, wrote out a check for $700, and handed it to Adrian. He drove Adrian home to Larchmont in his newly acquired car, answered a call of nature on our curb, and took off for Pelham, leaving his car in the Ramblers' parking field. The next morning, a peaceful Sunday, the phone rang. I answered it. It was Whiteman's wife. She shouted over the phone, "Tell Adrian to get his God-damned car off my lawn!" When Adrian awakened at noon I relayed the message to him. He promptly dressed and went to Whiteman's home, returned the check, and retrieved his car.

Around this time Adrian picked up two unusual novelty instruments. The Couesnophone, which he nicknamed the "Goofus," was an instrument made of brass which was held in the position of a flute; its neck curved inwards and the mouthpiece had an oval hole. However, it had a small piano keyboard with brass buttons for keys. It sounded like a cross between a harmonica and an accordion. The other instrument, which Adrian called the "Fountain Pen," was an elongated tube made of Grenadilla wood

approximately a foot long with a small mouthpiece like that of an
E♭ clarinet. This instrument had a series of holes and no chro-
matic keys—the chromatics had to be played by fingering half
holes. The sound was not unlike that of an E♭ clarinet, but with
far shorter range. Adrian made many recordings with these
instruments.

My sister Vera was a red-headed Italian with a fiery temper and
a stubborn attitude. Adrian and I were just the opposite. We
were peace-loving men, never quarreled with anyone, and just
enjoyed life. There was an incident one time when Vera was just
about to finish her second year of high school. My dad kept a very
strict dinner table, always saying grace before the meal. Vera
started an argument with me. I may have said something to
arouse her, I do not remember, but suddenly a fork flew across
the table and imbedded itself in my thumb. I still bear the scar to
this day. That incident resulted in Dad's sending her to finishing
school.

In the first year of high school I found the going a little more
difficult with the hard BA entrance course. I seldom took a book
home, however, but did my work during study period, and I
always sat in the front row in all my classes. In math I had to sit in
the front row. Mr Manchester was deaf and half blind, although
he was a good teacher. He would mumble almost inaudibly. The
boys in the last few rows were having a field day. They would run
about the class, throw paper airplanes, shout and yell. Mr
Manchester paid no heed; he just continued to mumble.

I borrowed Vera's alto sax, which she had played at school,
bought a few exercise books and started to play. After all, I could
read music well by now, with the help of Mr Conklin. I enrolled
in the Ernst Conservatory of Music in the Bronx, where I studied
clarinet with Professor Ernst, a former first clarinet player with
the Boston Symphony Orchestra. Three days a week I took the
Boston and Westchester Railroad for only a few cents and in less
than half an hour reached the school. Professor Ernst taught me
personally. My mother had bought me a Bundy metal clarinet,
which I used throughout high school.

Shortly, I formed a group of two saxes, piano and drums. It is
amazing the amount of work we got on weekends at $6 per man. I
had older boys or men working with me. Finally I got a call for a

fraternity dance at a college in the Bronx and went overboard and charged $7 per man. That night Meyer Davis was playing opposite us at another fraternity dance. They had a violin player in their group. I believe union scale was $14 per man at that time.

In my second year of high school Mr Conklin formed the banjo-mandolin band, actually a jazz group in disguise. I started to write a few things. Mr Conklin placed me in the male barbershop quartet, where I sang second tenor. I also sang in the glee club and played clarinet in the concert orchestra, Mr Conklin conducting. Sid Antonowski was the concert master.

During this year my dad developed cancer of the stomach. Mom was distraught. They went to specialists everywhere and Dr Cantle would visit the house daily, on foot. Dad found it difficult and his beautiful workmanship began to deteriorate. He was trying his best to work at home. He lost a lot of weight and suffered some pain. Dr Cantle suggested to Mom that he should see a surgeon. Mom contacted Dr Sinnett, a ruddy faced Irishman. After taking tests, which were not as extensive as they are today, an operation was planned to re-route the entrance to the stomach. Mom and Dad went to the hospital in Mount Vernon, New York, and, after preparation, the operation was performed. Dad rallied and seemed to be recovering. He resumed his work at home and in the summer of 1927 we went up to our summer home, again renting both houses.

One day, some time before, the Ramblers had a double session at the Thomas A. Edison recording studios. The boys had worked late the night before and, although they arrived at the Edison Studios promptly at 9 a.m., they were very tired. Edison asked them, "What's the matter with you fellows?"

Adrian replied, "We're tired, we worked late last night."

Edison declared, "All *I* need is four hours sleep." The boys finished their morning session and went to lunch. When they went back to the studio for the afternoon session, there was Thomas Alva Edison fast asleep with his feet propped up on his desk!

This was Prohibition time and the Ramblers Inn was inspected often for liquor. None could be found, but the officers saw that most people were drinking, and some of them were even intoxicated. The liquor was secretly kept in the trunk of Adrian's sports roadster and one night, after work, the federal men followed his car. Adrian put on a burst of speed and outran them. He was staying at home in Larchmont at that time. He came in panting with exitement.

During the earlier part of 1927 Adrian left the Ramblers and Ed Kirkeby, his partner and manager, took over the band. During the summer of 1927 I subbed a few times on third alto. I was only fifteen years old and so was Irving (Babe) Russin, who played fine tenor sax. Pee Wee Russell was on first alto and sometimes when he wasn't there a fellow by the name of Montgomery played first alto with a big, fat tone. Herbie Weil was playing drums; Jackie Russin, Babe's older brother, played magnificent piano. Spencer Clark played bass sax. I think that Bill Moore was still on trumpet, but sometimes it was Frankie Cush.

After a couple of brief rehearsals Adrian opened at the New Yorker Club with his all-star group. This band consisted of Bix Beiderbecke and Sylvester Ahola on trumpets and Bill Rank on trombone. The saxes were Bobby Davis, first alto, Frank Trumbauer, third sax, and Don Murray on tenor sax and jazz clarinet. Joe Venuti the great jazz violinist and his partner Eddie Lang were there; Frank Signorelli played piano and Chauncey Morehouse was on drums. Adrian played bass sax.

One Saturday I went down to rehearsal with Adrian and was taken back by the sound of this great band. The arrangements were provided by Bill Challis, a fine writer. I marveled especially at the great sound of Bix. During a break he sat at the piano and played extraordinarily well. In the afternoon I went home jubilant, with the sound of this happy music still ringing in my head. That night I tuned in to their radio program. The band was superb, although all I had was a two-tube radio set which I had built myself. But there were few customers in the club, and this great band finished after a short run of about two months.

I was now in my third year of high school and admired a girl who was one year ahead of me. Her name was Claire Wemblinger, and she was a fine school actress. She had rehearsed a particular play in which she played the female lead. In one of the opening scenes she sat motionless within a picture frame, and after a long time she stepped out. She was just beautiful and I fell in love with her from a distance. When the play was over I applauded vigorously, until my hands reddened. This girl had the sexiest speaking voice that I had ever heard. For assembly Mr Conklin asked me to play a solo. I chose Jimmy Dorsey's *Oodles of Noodles*. At the conclusion I saw Claire applauding the same way that I had for her, and we had a mutual admiration society going. The previous summer I had seen her at the beach, wearing a blue bathing suit which contrasted perfectly with her golden hair. She was always surrounded by boys and I did not dare to approach her.

There were other girls that I liked at Mamaroneck High. One was Lillian Piccoli, our jazz pianist, who sat in front of me in one of my classes. I went to her home a few times with my horn and we jammed. Lillian was good. Another girl that I liked in high school was Helen Lindsay, who sat across the aisle, one seat forward. She was a pretty brunette with a large bust. I invited her to the junior prom. Maybe it wasn't the prom, for I was wearing a heavy coat. (They don't have proms during the winter that I know of.) However, I picked Helen up at her home and we went to the dance. At the dance she looked very pretty but we hardly spoke. She got sidetracked with some boys and I with another girl. Someone else drove Helen home and I drove the other girl home. I do not know to this day whose date she had been.

It was late in the year, possibly November, when Adrian was summoned to go to England. He was to take three American boys and join Fred Elizalde's band at the Savoy Hotel in London. Adrian chose Bobby Davis (alto sax), Sylvester Ahola (trumpet) and Chelsea Quealey (jazz trumpet). After going through the usual routine of passports, etc, they set sail for Europe. Adrian did well in London financially and Fred Elizalde, a sugar millionaire's son, treated him exceptionally well. The Savoy Hotel was on a par with the Waldorf Astoria here, and the Prince of Wales was a steady customer.

We were now into 1928. Dad had taken a turn for the worse the previous fall and could no longer work. By Christmas he was confined to his bed and Dr Cantle came daily to give him relief with an opiate. Mom stayed by his bedside constantly in order to respond to his every little wish. Dr Cantle sometimes came twice a day. Finally Mom cabled Adrian, telling him to return immediately. Adrian took the first ship out of England and arrived home on April 3rd. Dad was in a terribly weakened condition by now.

Adrian phoned Dixie, his fiancée, and she was ready when he arrived to pick her up. He drove her back to our house and they both entered Dad's room. Adrian asked, "Dad, can you hear me?" Dad nodded affirmatively. Adrian said, "Dad, this is Dixie. I want to marry her, do I have your blessing?" Dad put out his hand. Adrian bent down and Dad's hand brushed his face and he nodded in the affirmative again. Adrian kissed his father on the cheek and departed with Dixie. They had a lot to talk about. It had been such a long time. Adrian and Dixie were married on 6 April 1928.

During the night of April 14th Dad grew weaker and we kept a steady vigil. The next morning, a Sunday, the Baron was dead. Mom took it extremely hard and became hysterical. Dr Cantle was summoned and gave her an opiate to calm her. Adrian, Vera and I made funeral arrangements. Dad already had a family plot for six in Kensico Cemetery in Valhalla, Westchester County, New York. He was laid out in our spacious living room after the undertakers had finished their work upstairs. The house was quiet. I could hear Mom sobbing in another room. The only sound in the living room was the little clock on the mantel which ticked away and gonged softly on the hour and half hour, its little pendulum still beating back and forth in perfect rhythm.

After the funeral Adrian and Dixie packed their bags and took the *Homeric* to England. The voyage was to be their honeymoon. I got back to my school work and musical studies, and in June 1928 was promoted and became a senior. I also continued to do club dates as leader but with the same pay as my sidemen.

That summer Mom again rented both houses and we went to stay at our summer home upstate. At the end of the holiday the people in the big house wanted an extension on their lease and Mom granted it. This meant that I would be late starting school again. I hated this because it meant cramming to catch up. One year I didn't get back to school until December 4th and had to work very hard. I went back to school in October, managed to catch up, and was back to normal again. I had just finished rehearsal with our jazz group one day when Mr Conklin rushed in. He said, "Arthur, I am ten minutes short on assembly time and need you to fill in."

I asked him, "What am I supposed to do?"

He said, "Lecture!"

"Lecture about what?" I inquired.

He answered desperately, "Anything—talk about the clarinet!"

I was to go on stage in two minutes. I had nothing prepared. Finally I was on stage with my metal Bundy clarinet and jabbered away for more than ten minutes. They almost had to get a hook to get me off.

Time went on and it was soon January 1929, my last semester. I was doing pretty well when Mom got a cablegram from Adrian, saying that he was coming home with Manuel "Lizz" Elizalde, Fred's older brother, to pick up additional American men. They chose Fud Livingston and Max Farley on saxes, both good arrangers. I had been practicing in the den and Lizz heard me. He said to Adrian, "What about the kid?"

Adrian replied, "He's going to school." They called me out and asked me if I would like to go to England. With mixed emotions I conceded. I really did want to graduate and go to Columbia University, but on the other hand I did not want to lose this opportunity. I also wanted to help Mom out financially. There were no concrete health plans then, to my knowledge, and the doctor's bills had mounted steadily during Dad's illness. There were also the expenses of the funeral and the surgeon, and Mom had very high taxes to pay. Vera was now working at a bank in New York City but Mom was feeling the pinch of not having had a real breadwinner for the past three years. I signed a one-year contract, and help out I certainly did, sending three-fifths of my salary home.

This is where my "Thirty Years" actually begins.

TWO

With Fred Elizalde in Europe

On 9 March 1929 we set sail for England on the *Berengaria*, which was the second largest ship in the world, of some 52,000 tons displacement. It was a terribly rough voyage and many of the people were sick in their cabins. I was sitting alone at a table in the lounge when a man came by and sat down with me. I introduced myself and asked his name. He said he was George Burns. I had never heard of him before. He invited me to play a game of checkers and we played several games. He told me that he and his wife had a vaudeville act. I told him that I was going to the Savoy and then asked, "Where is your wife?"

He answered, "In the cabin." Our table was pitching violently and I had to put some water on the tablecloth to make the checkerboard adhere. We met there again the next night, which wasn't so rough, and played a few more games.

During the daytime the boys took out their horns and we rehearsed a head arrangement on *Nobody's Sweetheart*. A few days out it was time for the ship's show and George Burns volunteered to be the MC. I never had so many laughs in all my young life; he was indeed a funny man. We went on with *Nobody's Sweetheart*, and there were a couple of other acts too. The rest of the trip was uneventful and we reached Le Havre, France, where Hal Fillis, Fred Elizalde's manager, met us. We then sailed across the channel to Southampton and on to London by train.

I moved in with Adrian and Dixie temporarily and ordered a new Selmer clarinet from Lewins Music Store. It was to have all the extra keys, including a low E♭. We had a rehearsal the next day and I marveled at this great orchestra, which included strings, and a harp played by Mario Lorenzi, also a good jazz harpist. I was only a kid, barely seventeen years old, and was awed by the talents of Fred Elizalde, who was only twenty-three years old himself—a Cambridge graduate who played fantastic piano and arranged brilliantly. The orchestra was truly superb, resembling Paul Whiteman's great orchestra in the USA.

The first night on the job I was wearing my father's tux, which had been altered and fitted to me, but it had a braid running along the lapels. Although this has become quite fashionable in later years it really wasn't in 1929. Bobby Davis, who was sitting next to me and playing first alto sax (I was playing tenor now, having bought a new horn before leaving New York), turned to me and, seeing the braided lapels, said tactlessly, "Kid, that tux has to go." I was embarrassed, to say the least. After the first set I called Adrian aside and told him about the tux. He said, "It looks good, kid, but if you feel uncomfortable, I'll lend you my spare tux, which is almost new." We were exactly the same size. The next night I wore Adrian's spare tux with an English vest and Bobby didn't bother me any more.

For the tea sessions, which were programmed for 4 to 5:30 p.m., the orchestra was split in two, each half alternating every other week. Adrian led one group and Bobby Davis the other. I was with Adrian's group, which he led with his bass sax up front. I played first alto on this. After the first week on the job George Hurley, the first violinist, approached me and asked, "Did you get your screw yet?"

I queried, "What do you mean George?"

He replied impatiently, "Did you get paid yet?" The British had many unusual expressions which I learned daily. Later, when I moved into the Shelbourne Hotel, where they had no room phones, I wanted to leave a call to be awakened. At the desk they asked, "What time do you want to be knocked up?"

On the first of April, when I came home from shopping, Adrian handed me a slip of paper with a telephone number on it. He said, "Lewins called. Your clarinet is ready." I hastily called the number written on the slip and said, "Hello, is this Lewins?"

The voice, a hollow one, answered "Yes," in a drawn-out tone.

I quickly queried, "Is my clarinet ready?"

The voice answered, "What clarinet?"

I became impatient and said, "The clarinet that I ordered."

He repeated, "What clarinet?"

I asked, "Is this Lewins?"

He answered, "Yes."

I was desperate by now and demanded, "Is this Lewins Music Store?"

He replied, in the same hollow voice, "No, this is Lewins Mortuary."

Adrian and Dixie broke up with laughter and Adrian said quietly, "April fool, kid!"

I stayed with Adrian and Dixie exactly two weeks and then I moved to the Tuscan Hotel. This was not a fancy place, but pleasant. The rate was $3 per day, which was rather expensive at that time. I considered it rather high and discussed it with Billy Mason, our pianist. Billy said, "Why don't you come to the Shelbourne Hotel where my wife and I are staying?" He went on, "It is only $18 a week for a single room with board and you have free access to the tennis court, billiard room, music room and ping-pong room." I stayed at the Tuscan Hotel exactly three days and then packed. I went down to the desk and said, "I'm checking out." They all laughed. I inquired, "What's so funny?"

They said, "We have never heard of that expression, checking out."

I was impatient and demanded, "What should I say?"

The clerk, a girl, replied, "You should say, 'Give me my bill, I am moving'."

I paid my bill and took a cab to the Shelbourne Hotel uptown. I moved in with my steamer trunk. I had lost the key and asked a handyman if he could open it. He said, "Easy." He then took a hammer and smashed the lock. They had given me a large room on the second floor overlooking the tennis court. There was a huge fireplace on one side which contained a gas heater. This heater had to be fed by English pennies, which were about the size of our old silver dollar but were worth about two cents. They were made of copper.

The British people had many coins to contend with and in the beginning I was a little confused. There was the farthing, worth half a cent, which I rarely saw. The halfpenny (pronounced "haypny") was worth one cent; the penny (pence if you had more than one), worth two cents; threepence (thrupnce), worth six cents; sixpence (sixpnce), worth twelve cents; shilling, worth a quarter; two shilling piece, worth fifty cents; and half crown, worth sixty cents. There was the pound, which was worth $5.00 in my book (actually $4.84 then), and the guinea, worth twenty-one shillings and rare. I would walk down the street with a load of change and didn't know which end was up. If you wanted to go to Woolworths, you would have to say, "Where is the nearest thrupnce and sixpnce store?" If I had an abundance of pennies they would weigh me down and I would walk sideways!

Back at the Shelbourne Hotel I was introduced to my table-mates Norman Webster and his sister Pat, who turned out to be lovely people. Norman was a stockbroker, who I later learned was earning just a little more than half my salary; I do not remember whether or not Pat worked. There was also a fourth person, a man whose name I never did know. Our waitress was Alice, a cute blond girl. The first night Norman, Pat and I chatted at the dinner table and they nicknamed me "jazz baby."

After the meal, which was exceptionally good, I had to dress for work. I took a cab to work and enjoyed the delightful sounds of the great orchestra. After work Billy Mason and I took a cab back to the Shelbourne Hotel. I ordered a cup of tea and fruit cake. The tea was almost as black as coffee and kept me awake for three hours that night. In the morning I had breakfast in bed, anything I wanted—eggs with bacon or sausage, or pancakes, or anything else I desired—and all for only $18 per week. I blessed Billy Mason.

Things were going well at the Savoy. Just like Adrian had said, the Prince of Wales came in often, and one night he asked to sit in on drums. Ronny Gubertini relinquished his seat and the Prince started to play. He was, let us put it this way, not too good. We bore with him and after the set he sent us two cases of champagne. That night I felt a little high from the champagne, for I had never drunk before. I felt OK when we finished, however.

The next day I contacted Sam Harris, the exquisite tailor who custom made all of Adrian's suits, and he came over with bolts of English worsteds and his equipment. I picked out a pattern that I liked and he went to work measuring me. All in all, he would take three fittings for each suit and they cost me only $40 per suit, now worth well over $500. I had suit after suit tailored, including one that cost only $36. He tailored a tux and overcoat for me for $40 each. I bought a cane and dark hat also.

Adrian had always been decidedly accident prone. He had inadvertently smashed cars, stepped into holes and, although he was not a clumsy person, frequently tripped. It was so bad that insurance companies refused him coverage. Eventually, even his death was the result of an accident: it happened in Florida when he fell down a flight of stairs into a pit of coral rock.

One night I was at the Savoy Hotel a little early and took my place on the bandstand. Adrian walked in with both arms wrapped in bandages. He had had to cut the sleeves off his tux. I asked, "What happened?" He explained that he and Dixie had gone out on a picnic in the countryside that afternoon and that he had decided to climb a tall tree. He was on the way down and near the bottom when the limb he was standing on broke, and he had to shinny the rest of the way down with both arms around the trunk of the tree.

On another night, after work, Adrian, two of the English boys and I went to Fred's apartment and we stayed there until about 6 a.m. It was situated on top of a steep hill on a side road parallel to the main road. Adrian spotted some bicycles against the building next-door. He didn't know about the English hand brakes, because at that time our brakes were controlled by reversing the foot-pedal action. He jumped on a bike and sped down the hill. He reversed the action of the foot pedals and his feet were working feverishly. At the bottom of the hill were several filled garbage cans. He plowed full force into the cans and flew up in the air and down again amidst a pile of garbage. We all laughed at the sight. He groaned groggily, "No brakes."

Adrian was hurt. We rushed him to a hospital emergency room. The doctor looked at him and said, "Are you here again?" He took several stitches in Adrian's eyebrow and we took him home. This time he was in bed for three days with bad bruises. While he was in bed he wrote a beautiful arrangement for the orchestra, without even a piano to assist him; his perfect pitch served him well. At the end of the week he received his full salary from Elizalde, plus the fee for the arrangement.

I gave up waiting for Lewins to deliver my clarinet and ordered one from Lafleurs. It was delivered on April 24th and was excellent. We started rehearsals a couple of days later for an opening at the Palladium Theatre on April 29th, meanwhile doubling at the Savoy. The show, a long one, consisted of several acts, one of which was "Lamb Chops" with my acquaintance from the *Berengaria*, George Burns. This was truly a funny act, the funniest that I had ever seen. George was the "comic" in those days and Gracie the "straight man." We howled at every performance, and George was frequently ad-libbing. We had to play three shows a day, plus both tea session and late evening session at the hotel. I averaged between nine and eleven taxi cabs per day.

After two weeks the show closed, and Fred Elizalde persuaded Dixie to let Adrian go to Brussels, Belgium, with Lizz Elizalde, Hal Fillis (our manager) and myself. We took off from the field early the next morning in a Fokker plane. It was very foggy and we could see nothing, so the pilot returned to the field and we waited for the fog to lift. We took off again and the Channel was beautiful; I could see the French coast clearly. This was my first experience in a plane and I was thrilled.

After we landed we headed for the Astoria Hotel, which had nice accommodations. I slept two hours and we went to Harry's Bar and met some of Adrian's old friends. We saw a revue and went to some nightclubs. My high-school French came in handy and I was the interpreter for our group. At one nightclub I had to go to the men's room. As I stood in front of the urinal I found it difficult to perform because there was a woman attendant standing just a foot behind me. This is common practice over there.

During the course of the evening I drank two bottles of champagne and felt a sense of euphoria. We returned to the hotel and retired at 5:30 a.m., after visiting Brussels's best brothel. This was my first experience with sex. I awakened at two o'clock in the afternoon with a head like a balloon. I proceeded to dress slowly, meanwhile thinking, "If sex does this to you, I don't want any part of it." I was soon to find out differently, however!

Back in London, on June 14th we had our first rehearsal for a concert that we were to play on June 23rd. It contained a difficult symphonic arrangement written by Fred Elizalde. We continued to rehearse while doubling at the Savoy. Three days before the concert Fud Livingston and Chelsea Quealey did not appear at rehearsal. It was a terrible thing for them to do just before the concert. Elizalde hired Jack Thurston, first clarinet player of the London Symphony Orchestra, to play Fud Livingston's chair. We later found out that Fud and Chelsea had returned to the USA. On the day of the concert we rehearsed all morning at Shepherd's Bush Pavilion for a two o'clock start. We played several jazz arrangements together with Fred's symphonic creation. Adrian and I got the most applause, although my horns needed adjustment.

We finished at the Savoy on July 31st, and on August 3rd I left for vacation with Norman Payne. He was a boy my age, seventeen, who played magnificent trumpet, resembling the style of Bix Biederbecke closely. Adrian loaned us one of his cars, a new American Essex, and we went to Brighton, Bournemouth, Teignmouth and Salcombe, ending up in Shoreham, where we remained for twelve days. When we returned to London and I found I did not have to work until the early part of September, I picked up my check and took a train back to Shoreham for another week.

Late in August Adrian and Dixie visited Holland, where Adrian was accorded the welcome of a visiting dignitary, and they were treated royally by the Dutch fans led by Max Goyarts, a fine musician. This was all illustrated in the fall 1977 edition of the magazine *Dr Jazz*, a Dutch publication. Adrian and Dixie returned from Holland and I viewed his films. They were excellent.

I went back to my old routine of having breakfast in bed with a waiter attending. One morning there was a knock at the door and I answered, "Come in." My little blond waitress, Alice, walked in with the tray, set it down on the dresser and came over to my bed. She kissed me . . . Alice and I became fast friends. She would sneak up a back stairway to my room nightly, fearing being caught. We would spend hours together and she would sneak out carefully.

We did a recording session, two sides, one of which was *Nobody's Sweetheart* with the small band, which we had rehearsed on the *Berengaria* in March. This was my first recording ever. Bobby Davis took the first half of a chorus and I picked him up for the second half. Adrian played brilliantly. The other side was *Singapore Sorrows*, which Fud Livingston had arranged and which contained a few bars of the magnificent trumpet playing of Norman Payne, my seventeen-year-old buddy. This little solo in Bix's tradition still stands up today.

We had an impending road tour through Scotland. We did a lot of packing and went for a short rehearsal to go over our new charts. On the night of September 1st we boarded the train, and when we awakened the next morning we were in Scotland. I could have slept more. We arrived in Glasgow and tried to get in a hotel, but there was a convention in town and we had trouble. We finally found accommodations at the Grand Hotel and then had a short rehearsal at the Palais de Dance.

That night the band went over very big. We played a lot of jazz arrangements and were besieged by Scottish musicians, who took us to our hotel and asked many questions. The next morning we took the early train for Aberdeen, a distance of about 155 miles, and we made it in four hours. Some of us checked into the Palace Hotel and others into the Grand Hotel across the street. That night we played at a small palais. The crowd was not big, but very enthusiastic, though the audience was better the following day. The next night we played a charity concert at the Music Hall, and on September 3rd we headed for Edinburgh. Upon arrival I looked around me and saw mountains and a castle overlooking this beautiful city. Jack Collins, the trombone player, and I took a room at the North British Hotel, the most exclusive in the city. That night we played at the Dunedin Palais de Dance and we had a good crowd. On the way back to London we stopped off at Leeds, and arrived home on October 3rd.

The following day I went to the office and collected my check for the Scotland tour and then I loafed. I saw Alice at the dinner table and we resumed our relationship that night. Sometimes we would meet at a pre-arranged place and would go back to the Shelbourne, she sneaking up after me.

In mid-November we started rehearsals for a Pola Negri soundtrack for a talking picture. Fred wrote the score. After two days of rehearsals we started to record. This work was tedious and we often worked from ten o'clock one morning to four o'clock the next. Shortly we caught up with Fred's score and he would often sit up writing after work for the next day's recording session. Fred looked haggard with no sleep; he was working around the clock.

We finished the soundtrack on December 2nd, and the orchestra was booked for another tour of Scotland starting on December 5th. Adrian did not go on this tour, but stayed behind to attend to Elizalde's affairs. I also stayed behind. The Home Office was wondering what a seventeen-year-old punk American was doing replacing an English musician.

Meanwhile, Alice and I played records at night, including Benny Goodman's magnificent solo on *Waitin' for Katie*, which he had recorded with Ben Pollack's band, and also some of Red Nichols's recordings. Then one night Alice did not appear. She must have been caught, for I never saw her again. I was saddened. I loafed some more. We had a new waitress now at our table, a brunette, but she was not like Alice.

It was about the third week in December 1929 when the stock market crash actually affected us. Although the crash had occurred on October 29th, it took that long for the shock waves to hit England fully. One day during that week I picked up my check as usual and went to the bank to cash it. The teller explained that the bank could no longer cash our checks because Elizalde's funds had been frozen. I called Adrian immediately and he told me that he had cashed his check just one hour before. When I told him my story he said, "Pack up, kid, we're going home." I told him that I didn't have enough funds. He added, "Don't worry, kid, I'll take care of your passage." He made the arrangements, and we left England on the following day on the largest ship at that time, the *Leviathan*, of some 54,000 tons displacement.

While I had been in England I had admired the work of Joe Crossman, an alto saxophonist who played with Bert Ambrose, as well as Norman Payne, Laurie Payne and Madge Mullen. She played piano and sang, and was featured by Ambrose. She was my age, too. We jammed one night and I was highly impressed. With Elizalde we had a trombone player by the name of Frank Coughlan, whom I also admired. Anyway, Adrian, Dixie and I steamed home and arrived in New York on Christmas Eve. Mom had rented the two houses in Larchmont, the summer place was closed for the winter, and she had taken an apartment downtown on Lafayette Street which my cousin, Maxmillian Cianfarra, had evacuated. My cousin Maxmillian was an immigrant and a sports reporter for an Italian newspaper. I had taught him the game of baseball the previous year, when we often went to the New York Yankee games and sat in the press-box. I was home now, but the two other American boys who had been in England with us, Bobby Davis and Max Farley, were stranded and remained so for over a year.

THREE

The California Ramblers, Bert Lown, Paul Whiteman and George Olsen

I did not know what to do at first, so I called Ed Kirkeby, Adrian's partner and the manager of the California Ramblers. He told me that he had the I. J. Fox (the furrier) radio program signed for thirteen weeks on WMCA, and asked me if I would like to do it. I said, "Yes." He told me that I would have to join Local 802, Federation of Musicians in New York. So I arranged for a test and, on the appointed day, went to 802 with my alto sax. The board had arranged to have me play some music which was on a music stand in the room. With the board listening, I delved into Mendelssohn's *Spring Song*, which was on top. I had known this selection and started to play it with ease. Suddenly one of the members called out, "Stop!"

I asked, "What's the matter?"

He replied, "Nothing, kid, just go down to the cashier and give him fifty bucks and you will get your card." I was relieved.

I did this radio show on Sundays and club dates in between, and also a few recordings with Adrian, who was now with Bert Lown at the Biltmore Hotel in New York.

Late in 1930 Ed Kirkeby called me and told me that we were opening at Will Oakland's Terrace on 51st Street, between Broadway and Seventh Avenue. The band was to consist of three saxes, trumpet, drums, bass, piano, and violin, with Jack Wechsler leading on the last-named. Herbie Weil, the drummer, who years later had a desk job at Local 802, suggested that we stay at the Victoria Hotel, which was practically across the street. We inquired as to the rates, double occupancy, and they quoted $18 per week, which meant $9 apiece. This sounded good and we moved into a large airy room on one of the upper floors. Herbie and I ate breakfast and luncheon at the B & G coffee shop on Seventh Avenue, diagonally across the street. There was an attractive hostess there, whose name I do not remember, but we chatted daily. Coffee then was ten cents for a bottomless cup, as they called it. It was delicious.

We worked long hours, from 6 p.m. to 3 a.m. There were two floor shows nightly and we had one half-hour break to eat dinner between 8:30 and 9 p.m. Herbie and I would order our dinner during an earlier ten-minute break and it would be ready for us promptly at 8:30. This was at the La Salle Restaurant on the corner of 51st Street and Seventh Avenue. We had an eight-course meal which cost us only fifty cents and we each gave the waiter a ten-cent tip. After all, this was twenty percent, and the waiter was pleased.

We had Sundays off, thank God. Herbie would visit his family in New Rochelle and I would often visit my mother and sister in Larchmont. I started studying flute with Louis Rossi, who would come once weekly to our hotel at 11 a.m.; he would teach me in the bathroom while Herbie was trying to sleep. He never complained.

Herbie was an acquaintance of Claire Wemblinger, the actress I had known in high school. One day he bumped into her and learned she had studied acting at the American Academy and was now playing in a show on Broadway with William Gaxton. Her name was now Claire Trevor. This lovely girl once left a note in my mailbox, saying hello and stating her whereabouts, but, sadly, I never followed it through. Years later she co-starred with John Wayne in *Wagon Train*.

We worked hard at Will Oakland's, and the show was long. The main attraction was the Hartmans, a ridiculously funny dance act. Paul Hartman was a tall, good-looking blond man and Grace, his wife, was equally handsome. The master of ceremonies would announce them over the PA system as "Don Hispano Esposito and his wife." Paul and Grace would be sitting at a ringside table in full evening attire. The MC said, "Perhaps we can prevail upon this couple to do a dance routine for us." There was applause and they shone the spotlight on them. Paul would reluctantly rise, take his wife's hand, and lead her to the dance floor. The act started out seriously, with exquisite ballroom dancing. This soon became a farce, with Paul spinning Grace over his head and throwing her, sliding, about twenty feet or so away from him on the dance floor. Later in the act he would do a cigarette and handkerchief trick. He would walk along the ringside and find a man with a handkerchief in his breast pocket. He would invite the man to the floor, snatch his handkerchief out of his pocket, open it and place a lighted cigarette in the center and fold it up, waving his hand. He would carefully open the handkerchief and hold it up for everyone to see. There was a big hole in the center. The band played a chord for this ending. One night, when he snatched the handkerchief out of a man's pocket, a contraceptive flew out onto the dance floor. Everyone howled. Paul and Grace Hartman continued their hilarious act for many years, and I was saddened when Grace died. Paul did some motion-picture work after that and I do not know at present what became of him.

Bobby Davis, first alto sax man, was with us on this job, having returned from England after the crash. He had a beautiful tonal quality on alto and baritone sax. At the closing of the floor show Will Oakland would always sing a song in his remarkable lyric tenor voice. We continued at Oakland's until the summer of 1931, when the place was closed for the season.

We then opened at Will Oakland's Hunter Island Inn in Pelham, New York, with Adrian, who had left Bert Lown, as leader. The rest of the band remained the same, with Bobby Davis, Johnny Rude and myself on saxes, Chelsea Quealey on trumpet, Lew Cobey on piano, Noel Kilgen, guitar, Herbie Weil, drums and vocals, Carl Smith, bass, and of course Jack Wechsler on violin. I stayed at Larchmont for this one, driving my 1931 De Soto roadster to and from work, a distance of about ten miles. The beautiful summer passed quickly, marred by only one little incident. Adrian had his bass sax on a high stand in front of the band. One night it toppled over, bending it severely. I looked at him and he said, "Don't worry, kid, I have a spare."

At the end of the summer we headed back to Will Oakland's Terrace in New York City, and we opened sans Adrian. Herbie Weil and I got our old room back and resumed the grind, still working from 6 p.m. until 3 a.m.; I was now practising four-string guitar. We worked at Oakland's until June 1932, when the place closed. I was home in Larchmont only a few days when I got a call from Adrian. He said, "Kid, Ed Kirkeby and I are opening a club on Pelham Parkway in the Bronx. Would you like to be with me?" I assented. He went on to tell me that it would be called the New California Ramblers Inn.

We opened the latter part of June 1932, Adrian leading. This was basically the same combination that we had had at the Hunter Island Inn, but without Jack Wechsler, the violinist. We had a few arrangements and doctored-up stocks. Our opening night was dismal. We tried everything to please the small crowd. The inn had been beautifully decorated by Dixie, who spent many hours sewing the drapes, and we had tablecloths to match. The food was good, but little business.

During this period, Ed Kirkeby, Adrian's partner, invited people in free of charge, providing them with set-ups. Some would bring in their own liquor, for this was the height of Prohibition. Our bass player, George, an alcoholic, would wait for a party to leave and consume their dregs from their tables.

After one week Adrian became ill with a serious kidney ailment, and he was confined to his bed upstairs, Dr Martin, a kidney specialist, attending. In those days the miracle drugs were not as yet discovered and Adrian suffered. I took over as leader of the band, writing a few charts: still no business. After three weeks we received no pay, and the boys became impatient.

Isham Jones had opened across the street at the Pelham Heath Inn with a big band starring Saxie Mansfield on tenor. We could hear the beautiful sounds of that band; they were jammed, and we were dead.

Adrian was really sick and I would visit him regularly upstairs. Dixie seldom came down while attending him. Soon the boys were receiving small change as pay. I was receiving nothing. When the boys left the bandstand they would disappear to all parts of the property, and I would have trouble locating them. I did not blame them, because they were not being paid. Some of them had families. After about three weeks of this I had trouble with Teddy Sandow, our trumpet player (who played beautifully), and we almost had a fist fight when he refused to get on the stand. This was truly the depth of the Depression.

One night a beautiful, mature young lady walked in. She was blond and had a cute, trim figure. She went over to May, the

coat-room lady, and sat down. (May Kelsall, an English Canadian, had had the coat-room and ladies' room concessions in the
old California Ramblers Inn some few years back.) I asked May to
introduce me to her. She was hesitant at first, and finally introduced us saying, "Ena, I would like you to meet Art, the leader of
the band." We exchanged formalities and I was in love with this
girl at first sight.

That night, after the usual struggle, I took May and Ena home.
They were living in a small home on City Island, a few miles
away. May, hithertofore, had gotten rides from one of the
waiters, and she welcomed the change. On the way home she
explained to me that Ena was only fifteen years old and was to be
sixteen on September 9th. I was twenty and wore a mustache
now.

This procedure continued nightly for some time, when I asked
May if I could take Ena home alone. She hesitantly agreed and we
were off. I stopped at a speakeasy at Pelham Bay and invited her
in for a beer. She drank the beer eagerly and ate all the pretzels
and maraschino cherries in front of her. I could tell that she was
hungry; there was no other food at this establishment. I drove her
home promptly and dropped her off at the door, and asked,
"What is May to you?"

She replied, "Just a very good friend."

Back to the grind the next night. Ena was there, and at closing
time May allowed me to take her home again. We stopped off at
the same speakeasy and sat down at the bar and ordered beer,
Ena delving into the pretzels and cherries. The owner-bartender
exclaimed, "Young lady, I'm losing money on you." Ena stopped
eating, and we had three more glasses apiece of "needle ether"
beer, which was extremely potent. On the way back to City
Island Ena became violently ill and had me stop the car, throwing
open the door and retching violently. I did not feel so well myself
and we vowed never to go back to that place again.

I took Ena home nightly, never being allowed to kiss her. One
night May confessed that Ena was her daughter and that she had a
son, Billy, two years older almost to the day. I had not met Billy
because I was never allowed into their house up until this time.
I asked Ena about her dad. She told me that he was an actor,
having played in *Blossom Time* on the road; the last that she

had heard from him, he had a job as a singing waiter in a club and was unable to send money home. Times were tough then.

Things were also tough at the inn. Adrian was still very ill and the battles continued, the boys jingling loose change in their pockets. But we plowed on. Ed Kirkeby would come in weekly, usually on Friday nights, and try to liven things up. He would invariably call out, "My Gal Sal!" No response. Now Ed had many other interests in his booking office and found it extremely difficult to come to this place. He would stay only a short while. Finally he came in one night and announced that he had sold the club. I asked, "To whom?"

He replied, "Jimmy Baker."

I asked, "Who, the mobster?"

He replied quietly, "Yes."

The waiters and chef were discharged and Jimmy Baker, a good-looking man with an unhealthy pallor, took over, introducing new waiters and a chef, all of whom carried guns and knives. We could see the bulges in their pockets. May was still there. Business boomed on opening night, and the place was crowded with the underworld.

It was now September 1932. The second week that Baker was there he made passes at Ena and demanded that she go out with him. May came to her rescue and told him, "Keep away from my daughter." She shook her finger in his face with temper. Jimmy knew that I was seeing Ena. May told me all of this that night. I feared being bumped off!

The following week was coming to a close when I heard a rumor of an impending police raid. The boys carefully packed their instruments and departed. Ena, May and I stayed behind. Suddenly the police broke in. Jimmy Baker was gone, but they rounded up the waiters and the chef, searching them for weapons – of which they found many. They didn't bother the three of us at all. They searched the place for liquor and found none. I knew where the liquor was—it was hidden under a trapdoor covered by a rug under Adrian's bed. (Adrian was still in bed but rapidly recovering, and Dixie was upstairs with him.) The police emptied the place, padlocked the doors and left one side door open for Dixie to go marketing. I said goodbye to Adrian and Dixie and drove to Larchmont after dropping Ena and May off at their home.

I didn't do a single thing for a week, when suddenly the phone rang and it was Adrian. He said, "Kid, I am feeling OK now. Would you like to go with Bert Lown at the Park Central?"

I replied, "Fine. When?"

He said, "In a couple of days."

We opened at the Park Central Hotel. Lown was a handsome blond man, for whom I had done some college dates before. He was not a good musician, getting by mostly on his personality. The band consisted of Larry Tice on first alto, Bernie Gluckman on third alto, and myself on tenor, doing the solo work. The brasses were Eddie Petrowitz on first trumpet, Eddie Farley on second trumpet (later of Farley–Riley fame: *The Music Goes 'Round and Around*) and Al Philburn, one of our arrangers, on trombone. (Al made Chauncey Gray's *Bye-bye Blues* famous with his rendition of our closing theme which he had played at the Biltmore.) The rhythm section was Fulton "Fidgey" McGrath on piano, Tommy Felline on guitar, Stan King on drums and Merrill Kline on string bass, later followed by Spencer Clark on bass sax. He just played the bass notes with vibrato, and this irked Adrian a little. Adrian played vibes, chimes, solo bass sax and second trombone parts. Mac Ceppos was on violin. We had good air time and the band was very popular; one night Benny Goodman came in with a date to hear us. We also made some recordings for Perfect records and Bluebird, a poor man's Victor label.

Adrian was a boating enthusiast and owned a Chris Craft cruiser and speedboat and would often stay up all night. One night he fell asleep, his head on the vibes, and took a two-hour nap, though he awakened for the broadcast. Lown loved him. We finished this date in February 1933; our contract had expired, and we were replaced by a "Mickey Mouse" band.

I was walking down Broadway a few days later and bumped into Fud Livingston, who was working with Paul Whiteman at the Paradise Restaurant down the street. We exchanged greetings and he asked, "Art, how would you like to take my place with the 'Old Man'?"

I asked, "When?"

He replied, "I'll fix it tonight, and you can start tomorrow." I nodded in the affirmative and left him. Fud called me the next day at noon and declared, "Art, you start tonight."

Little did I know what was in store for me. The arrangements were difficult and we worked hard. Whiteman had me playing jazz flute at the mike and also jazz tenor. He nicknamed me Mousie because I never said anything. Two of the original Rhythm Boys were there, Harry Barris and Al Rinker, but Bing Crosby had left and Johnny Mercer the great lyricist had taken his place. Johnny was very talented and could go to a table and spontaneously rattle off a set of lyrics on any given song. Bennie Bonacio was on first alto. My memory does not serve me well as to a man on third sax E♭ alto; maybe there was none. Bullet Cordaro was on fourth sax, tenor, and jazz clarinet, and Charlie Strick-faden, the band treasurer, on baritone sax, english horn and oboe. The brass consisted of, I believe, Charlie Margulis on first trumpet, Charlie Teagarden as second trumpet and jazz soloist, and Bill Rank, Adrian's old sideman, on trombone (he was later replaced by Jack Teagarden). Bennie Bonacio, first alto and straight clarinet, went on vacation to Italy, stayed a little too long, and was replaced by Al Gallodoro.

I do not remember the string players' names except that Matty Malneck, a fine violin player (both concert and jazz) was there. Chauncey Morehouse was on drums and timpani and the old standby Mike Pingitore was on banjo and four-string guitar. As most people know, Mike was a cripple, having had polio in his youth, and wore a huge sole on one shoe. He was also the band librarian. Whiteman would often kid him and say, "Where do you keep all of your money, Mike, in your shoe?" And of course the great Roy Bargy, assistant conductor and arranger, was on piano.

We started at 7 p.m. and finished at three o'clock in the morning. We also did the "Old Gold" cigarette show. Whiteman paid me $150 per week, which was good for a twenty-one-year-old kid during the deep depression when meals were only fifty cents. Some adult people were earning only $15 to $20 per week.

Frank Trumbauer the great C-melody sax artist had left White-man and gone on the road with his own band. Whether or not he had the personality for it, I do not know, but he was fading fast. He had told Whiteman that if anything happened adversely, he would like his old job back. After six weeks he returned, a failure with his band, and played a guest shot on the "Old Gold" show. And he waited.

We had been doing various benefits for worthy causes and were extremely busy. We also recorded on Victor records for additional pay. I found myself working practically around the clock. One night Whiteman came to me and said, "Mousie, I want to speak to you." We went to one side of the bandstand and Whiteman continued, "I am very sorry to say this, Mousie, but I am going to have to let you go. Frank is coming back." He added, "Don't worry, I will take good care of you." I received my two-weeks' notice in the mail. This was a lengthy letter with Whiteman's caricature at the top.

Whiteman kept his promise, however. He was playing golf with George Olsen the day after I finished (Sunday), and recommended me as a replacement for Emmet "Irish" Callen, who did not want to go on the road. Olsen had a popular band at that time with his wife, Ethel Shutta, as vocalist. Olsen called me and we dickered over price. We finally came to an agreement and he asked me to go to the Pennsylvania Hotel the next afternoon for rehearsal. I met all of the boys, including Irish Callen, whom I was to replace. We rehearsed. Irish Callen, who was a good flute player, turned to me and said, "I'll trade you a cold flute for a hot clarinet." The saxes now consisted of Teddy Gompers on first alto, flute and bassoon, Henry Susskind on third alto, Hotcha Gardner, a handsome young man, on baritone sax and vocals, and myself on tenor and clarinet. I do not recall the names of the men on brass, although I do remember that Jimmy Zito was playing trumpet. Abe Pizik was on drums and Joe Rhodes on bass.

We headed for a theater in Buffalo, New York, the next day. We had to wear makeup on stage, so I bought the necessary equipment. Olsen would examine each of us backstage and check our makeup, carefully looking even behind our ears. He was an incredible perfectionist.

I heard from Ena. All that I had given her was my signet ring, but she hinted "engagement". I was not ready: after all, I was twenty-one and she was only seventeen. I wrote to her that I was not quite ready and would see her when I got home. She was dissatisfied and threw my ring out of the window of her home and took up with another boy for spite. I loved her, but was not quite ready for an engagement. I had responsibilities at home, and felt that I was too young.

We toured through the Middle West. No word from Ena. I played it cool and did not write. At one city I asked a bellhop to send up a call girl. I paid her in advance and we romanced. The next day was to be payday and I knew just how much money I had had in my wallet: $23. I awakened the next morning and found only $3. I immediately called the desk and told them. They were very kind, and told me that a pencil salesman had also been robbed and they would credit me for the $20. The next day George came to me and handed me $100 on account, saying that he would give me the rest the day after. The boys asked me if I had been paid. I replied, "Only partially. I got a hundred bucks."

They chorused, "A hundred bucks!" After all, this was the deep depression and money could buy a lot. I found out then that these men were earning less than $100 and that I was the highest-paid man in the band.

In the meantime Mom had rented all three houses and moved to an apartment on 161st Street and the Grand Concourse in the Bronx. I sent money home to her weekly, and she opened a savings account for me.

In this band we played band imitations and I was selected to play the clarinet cadenza on the opening of *Rhapsody in Blue*. This always went smoothly and I felt elated.

The sixth week, which was to be the last of the tour, we played a theater in St Louis. The time dragged although the reception was good. Just before the week ended Olsen announced that we were going to Texas at a cut in salary. I said, "No good, George. I was hired for six weeks and want to go home." I made the feeble excuse that Mom was ill and I had to leave. He seemed pleased at not having to pay my salary anymore and suggested, "I'll give you the fare to New York, but you can take a train to Chicago and a bus on to New York with my maid, and save money."

In Chicago we piled into a dirty bus (Indian Bus Lines). It was hot and humid and we progressed slowly on the poor roads. The bus constantly broke down and I craved a shower. Somewhere in Pennsylvania the bus quit for good. We waited, and finally a relief bus appeared. We piled in once again and continued the bumpy ride. The trip dragged on, the ride was rough, and I cursed Olsen silently. The roads were dusty and dirty, with many detours. We finally arrived in New York forty-five hours after our time of departure in Chicago, and with no sleep. I was completely spent. I went to 161st Street and slept for twelve hours straight. I was even too tired to eat.

I awakened the next day, had a late breakfast, and was sitting in my robe relaxing, when the phone rang. I answered it. "Hello," the voice stated, "this is Benny Goodman."

I said, "Hello, Benny, what's up?"

He said, "I'm going to rehearse a band for Billy Rose's Music Hall. Do you want to come down to rehearsal tomorrow?"

I said, "OK. What time?" He told me to be there at three o'clock and I agreed. I had known Benny slightly from when he had come to the Park Central Hotel when I was with Bert Lown, and he also had come to hear Whiteman at the Paradise Restaurant. And I had worked with him on recordings with Adrian, such as *Savage Serenade* and *Sweet Madness*, and others before that. He was a tremendous jazz giant.

FOUR

Joining Benny Goodman

At the first rehearsal with Goodman we played Edgar Sampson's *Stompin' at the Savoy* and several arrangements that Irving Szathmary had written. Billy Rose had hired Lou Foreman, a middle-aged man, to conduct the show. (Benny could not conduct.) The saxes consisted of Benny Kantor on first alto, Hymie Shertzer on third sax (and violin for the intended show) and yours truly on tenor sax. Eddie Wade was on first trumpet, Russ Case on second trumpet and Jerry Neary on third. (Sammy Shapiro later replaced Eddie Wade on first.) The trombones consisted of Jack Lacey on first and Red Ballard on second. Stan King was on drums (later replaced by Sammy Weiss), Claude Thornhill on piano, and Hank Wayland on bass.

We were to alternate with Jerry Arlen's band. (Jerry was the brother of Harold Arlen the songwriter.) Our band sounded terrible playing the show at rehearsal, so Billy Rose chose Arlen as the show band, which also played a little dance music. We became the dance band.

The Music Hall was a converted theater, the floor having been leveled, and the bands faced each other from either side of the stage end. We opened on 8 April 1934 with a fairly good crowd. Billy Rose was a writer of ballad songs, and it was plain to see that he did not appreciate jazz. We also had a seven o'clock broadcast several nights a week on WNEW and would go on "cold," so we were often out of tune. On Thursday evenings Benny would borrow Benny Kantor's tenor sax and play the "Chase and Sanborn" radio show, which he had rehearsed the same afternoon in the studios. Benny also used Kantor's tenor for some arrangements we played by Benny Carter that called for four saxes. We worked seven nights a week, from 7 p.m. until 3 a.m., at the lowest salary that I had ever worked. But I wanted to play in a swing band. I very seldom saw Ena, though once in a while I would meet her in the afternoon when we were not rehearsing.

Benny still had a contract with Columbia records and we did occasional dates. Every night he would play *The world is waiting for the sunrise*, and he played brilliantly every time. On the Columbia recording he played poorly compared to the way he played on the job. (It was called *Music Hall Rag* on the recording.) One day Benny and I were riding in a taxicab on the way to a Columbia recording session when he turned to me and said, "Art, some day I'm going to make $1000 dollars a week." In less than one and a half years he was actually earning many times that amount. In those days Benny had a Chicago accent. Years later he developed an affected Park Avenue "society" accent.

I had a lot to play and felt free to improvise any way that I chose, but a couple of years later Benny became more critical and would listen carefully to every note a man played. Then I felt restricted and often played the same jazz solos. So did Murray McEachern (trombone) and Red Ballard, who played only one trombone solo in the book. It was an almost straight solo on the first chorus of *Can't we be Friends?*, and he dreaded it. A year after Benny broke up his band I was working with Red Ballard with Richard Himber's band at the Palladium Ballroom in Hollywood. He played great jazz solos with great abandon, and I was amazed. The difference was that there was no pressure. Murray McEachern went with Whiteman and was featured both on alto sax and trombone; he sounded great.

One night I was sitting on the bandstand and, lo and behold, who was standing in front of the bandstand but Ena. She was wearing a very low-cut red blouse and short white skirt. She was carrying a tray of cigarettes with fresh flowers on the side. She had obtained the job from Harry Susskind, the concessionaire. She did fine for two weeks, making good tips, when one night a customer bought a package of cigarettes and a rose. He tipped her well and told her that she could keep the rose. She thanked him and promptly put it in one corner of her tray and went about her work. The rose had become partially wilted. She went back to Susskind's office for more cigarettes and Susskind noticed the rose in the corner of her tray. He queried, "What is that flower doing there?"

She answered, "It's been sold."

He said, "Sell it again."

She said, "I can't, it's wilted."

He demanded, "Sell it again."

She said, flatly, "I won't, I quit!"

Ena's stay was short-lived. She soon got a summer stock job singing and dancing with a show in New Jersey, across the Hudson River. I hadn't seen her for a month when one night I received a telegram saying that she would be in town that night. I wired back saying that I had made reservations for rooms at the Victoria Hotel, the old stamping ground from the time I had been working at Will Oakland's with the California Ramblers. Ena finished work in New Jersey and picked up her key at the desk and went to bed. She was very tired and retired rather early, but I had to work until three in the morning. I went to the hotel and picked up my key. Our rooms were a few doors apart. I took the elevator to our floor and stopped at her room and knocked lightly on the door. No answer. I knocked harder and harder. Still no answer. I went down to the desk and called her room on the house phone. Still no answer. I then went back up and knocked even harder.

While I was knocking I heard footsteps behind me. I turned around and there was the house detective. He took me by the arm and led me down to the desk in the lobby and was ready to arrest me. Fortunately the desk clerk remembered me from a few years earlier and he told him to let me go. We then went up to investigate. I stayed outside the door and he went in and found Ena sound asleep. He said to me, "You had better go to your room." I went to my room disgruntled.

Late the next morning I called Ena from the lobby and told her what had happened. I asked, "What did you do, take a bottle of sleeping pills?" She explained that she had been rehearsing the whole day before, then had worked the night show, and was exhausted. We had a late breakfast that morning and went to Central Park to row on one of the beautiful lakes. We took pictures and had a late lunch. Then she had to go back across the river to do her show and I had to dress for the Music Hall, so we parted.

We finished the engagement at the Music Hall on October

17th and on October 23rd we did the Decca recording with Adrian which was mentioned in the Fall 1978 issue of *Dr Jazz*. The personnel included Manny Klein (trumpet), who split the date with Bunny Berigan, Jack Teagarden (trombone), Benny Goodman (clarinet), Artie Bernstein (bass), Howard Smith (piano), George Van Eps (guitar), Stan King (drums), Adrian (bass sax) and myself (tenor sax). Adrian contracted the date, but I had the pleasure of asking Goodman to do it!

As we were unpacking our instruments Adrian turned to me and said, "Kid, I haven't touched my horn in three months." (He had been playing other instruments during this period.) It was plain to see that his reed was badly warped. He straightened the reed and we went in to a rundown of *Sugar*. All four sides were arranged by Fred Van Eps. After being paid union scale, which was $25 for a three-hour session then, Benny grumbled to me.

Meanwhile, Irving Kolodin, one of the men responsible for the hiring of bands for a three-hour "National Biscuit Show," suggested Goodman as the swing band on the show. Xavier Cugat was to be the Latin Band and Kel Murray the straight dance band, which was to be composed mostly of freelance musicians. We did a rehearsal, free. We did an audition free as well, and got our spot by only one vote.

On December 1st we did our first NBC show, called "Let's Dance," which was rebroadcast to the West Coast. Benny hired Toots Mondello and Dick Clark from the Joe Haymes band. Two days later I did a transcription for Frank Black, which paid more than the NBC show. Benny hired George Bassman, Spud Murphy, Fletcher and Horace Henderson and, later, Jimmy Mundy, to do the arranging, as well as Gene Krupa on drums, Bunny Berigan and Pee Wee Erwin, trumpets, and Buddy Clark and Helen Ward on vocals.

It was just a little before December that Adrian opened his Tap Room in the President Hotel. I had taken a room there in the hotel; Adrian had gotten me a good rate because he knew the owners. Ena was now home and Adrian wired her to work the coat room. She responded immediately and took a room in a brownstone building about three doors away from the President for $4 a week. It was cold now and there were plenty of hats and coats in the large coat room, and she also sold cigarettes. She got good tips which Adrian split with her.

Adrian was doing seven radio shows a week. He was bass sax guest soloist on the "Norman Claudier Show." He played a show called "Forty Flying Fingers" on piano with three other pianists. He played vibes, chimes and timpani on the "James Melton Show" and later was appointed official drummer of the orchestra when the regular drummer didn't show up. I bumped into him on 49th Street near the studio carrying a snare-drum case and asked, "Where in hell are you going with that?"

He answered, "I'm playing drums now, kid."

He was doing the "Studebaker" commercial transcriptions with Richard Himber three times a week, playing vibes, xylophone and chimes, plus another show that I cannot recall at the moment. Adrian had unusual stamina for he also worked at the Tap Room every night.

He told me an amusing story about Himber. Himber always hired top studio men for his dates, including Arnold Brilhart, Artie Shaw, Manny Klein and many other fine musicians. Perhaps Benny had played for him. After rehearsal one afternoon the boys set the studio clock five minutes ahead. To this day I have never seen this done, as the clocks are synchronized with the electric current and are accurate to the second. At the broadcast the men had their instruments poised and Himber gave a downbeat. No one played. He turned an unhealthy pallor and gave another downbeat. Still no response. He was desperate now and the men broke out laughing. Himber then realized that he had been tricked.

On another broadcast Adrian had a thirty-one-bar rest. He laid his head on the vibes and pretended to be asleep. Himber was perturbed and watched him carefully, but at the end of the thirty-one bars Adrian straightened up and played a chord.

At the Tap Room Fats Waller was pianist and entertainer. He would have drinks lined up above the keyboard on the upright piano and throw them down straight without batting an eye. He would consume over two quarts of whiskey a day. The Tap Room was the talk of the town. Crosby, Martha Raye, leading actors from both Hollywood and New York, went there almost nightly.

Wingy Manone and Joe Marsala followed Fats Waller with their groups. Adrian followed with his own group.

One night, while at the Tap Room, I happened to mention to Adrian that I was going to be in the Bronx the next afternoon. He said, "Kid, I bought a pawn ticket from a guy last night. Will you redeem it for me?" I told him that I would, and he pulled the ticket out of his wallet. It read: "Gibson guitar, $25." He handed the money and the ticket to me.

The next afternoon I stopped at this pawn shop and presented the ticket. The owner went to the back of the store and I waited, five, ten, fifteen minutes. I was growing impatient, when suddenly the front door opened and I felt a hand grasping my shoulder. It was a police detective. He demanded, "Where did you get that ticket?" I quickly explained the situation and identified myself, telling him that I was working with Benny Goodman on the "Let's Dance" show. The owner of the shop joined him and explained that several blank tickets had been stolen and that there was no guitar. They then let me go. That night I saw Adrian and told him the story. He nonchalantly said, "Clipped again!"

Dixie was running White Way Music, a drum shop on Broadway, where practically every drummer in New York shopped for equipment. Dixie constantly wound vibe mallets, even at home, for the numerous vibe players. Bill West was the drum teacher. One day Buddy Rich, a very young lad, came into town and headed for White Way. Adrian was impressed by his talent and was instrumental in getting him a job on 52nd Street.

For Christmas Day Benny had booked a one-nighter in Binghamton, upstate New York. To save money he chartered a four-cylinder Coney Island sightseeing bus for the trip. Coney Island is an amusement park on the ocean in the southern part of Brooklyn. The bus had never before been out of that area. We piled in carrying our own instruments (we didn't have a band boy then). Everything was fine until we got about thirty-five miles north of New York City, and then the bus had trouble climbing the hills. They became steeper and steeper and the driver was in low gear. Finally we all had to get out with our instruments and walk up the hills. We reached the top before the bus. This went on repeatedly, and it was terribly difficult for the drummer.

Benny found a telephone and called ahead, saying that we would be late. We finally arrived at the dance hall at 11 p.m., quite disheveled and perspiring profusely, even though it was winter. A girls' band was playing but we finished the date. Fortunately it was downhill going back to New York City and the bus made it easily. My records show that I did not get paid for this date.

Bunny Berigan had been with us for some time, and the band was now cooking. Fletcher Henderson continued to write, and we had new charts weekly. The saxes consisted of Toots Mondello on first alto, Hymie Shertzer on second alto, myself on first tenor and Dick Clark on second tenor. George Van Eps was on guitar.

One night Benny forgot our pay checks, and we had to drive out to Long Island to get them. Ethel Goodman, Benny's sister, was his secretary. It was bad enough that I had trouble finding the house, but upon handing me my check, she remarked, "What are you going to do with *all* that money?"

I answered, "What money?" I was still sending money to my mother, and did so for years and years to come. My sister couldn't work because she had a thyroid condition plus a bad eye nerve which caused migraine headaches.

The NBC show came to a conclusion on 25 May 1935 after running for twenty-six weeks. On June 6th, under the name of the Rhythm Makers, we accomplished an almost incredible feat of recording fifty-one arrangements in three hours for World Transcriptions. We ran through almost our entire library, just one time, with different men filling in the vocal parts with solos. Berigan was not on this date, and Pee Wee Erwin played the trumpet solos. We received a grand total of fifty-one dollars—one dollar per tune.

We opened directly at the Roosevelt Hotel, following Guy Lombardo. Although we had quite a few ballad-type charts in our library, and I warned Benny to take it easy and play softly, he paid no heed and barreled into *King Porter Stomp* at the dinner hour. The management had never heard anything like this before. The waiters were rattling dishes, knives and forks, and holding their fingers in their ears. As a result we played there for only two weeks: we received two weeks' notice on the first night!

In July we began our first national tour. I bought a new 1935 Ford Coupe, and Allan Reuss, who replaced George Van Eps on guitar, was my co-driver. (Van Eps and Mondello did not want to go on the road.) We took off for Pittsburgh, where we were to play the Stanley Theatre for two weeks while staying at the William Penn Hotel. Benny was a little perturbed with the fact that I could carry only two persons in my car, but after he obtained an auxiliary PA system, which I could carry in the trunk, he agreed to pay me three cents per mile, the same as the others with a back seat. We never had occasion to use the PA, however, as each hall had its own system. There was a PA, I recall, at Will Oakland's Terrace, when I was there with the California Ramblers, but Oakland used it only for announcements and his remarkable lyric tenor vocals, and never as a tool to amplify the band. Later, while at the Palomar Ballroom, Allan and I decided to visit Tijuana, Mexico, on a day off. We were admitted OK at the border, but on our return we were detained by the authorities when they opened the trunk and saw the PA. I explained the situation to them, and after phoning Goodman, who fortunately was in his motel, they released us.

After the first show at the Stanley Theatre I practiced on my own for a few minutes and then went down to the stage door to leave the theater. A lovely brunette greeted me. She asked if Benny were in the theater. I told her that all the boys had left. She was carrying a zippered black portfolio under her arm and said that she wanted an interview for a local newspaper. I said, "Perhaps I can help." After all, I had been with the band since its inception.

She queried, "Where are you staying?"

I said, "At the William Penn around the corner."

She said, "Let's go."

We walked to the hotel and took the elevator up to my floor. We entered my room and I asked her to be seated while I washed my hands. I went into the bathroom to answer a call of nature and wash my hands. I came out and to my utter surprise she was lying on the bed stark naked, her portfolio on the chair. I was both taken aback and shocked. Although she was beautiful, I could not get excited without at least some foreplay. I stood there a moment and told her to get dressed. The only clothing on the chair was a dress and there were shoes on the floor. I chatted while she dressed reluctantly. I said to myself, "What an interview!" She finally confessed that she was not a newspaper reporter at all, but a vocalist with a local band. Her name was Cora, and she was a nymphomaniac. She confessed to me that she could never get enough sex. I dismissed her and went back to the theater and practiced some more.

When we first reached Pittsburgh Benny had called a rehearsal in a studio upstairs in the theater. He auditioned Bill De Pew on third sax (alto and clarinet) with the whole band standing around. When Bill played clarinet Benny exclaimed excitedly, "He sounds like me!" He was hired. Bill, who had been extremely nervous, now sighed a great sigh of relief and smiled.

We did many one-nighters on the way to Denver, Colorado, where we were to open at Elitche's Gardens, a dime-a-dance place. We were booked there for three weeks. However, it was plain to see that we were a flop. Our NBC program had not reached Denver and, although the band sounded great, we were not being accepted. The manager wanted us to play waltz sets in between the regular sets and Benny was disheartened. He split the band into two groups for the waltzes and we faked the numbers, alternating with each half. Helen Ward, our vocalist, was playing piano and Jack Lacey, trombone, was on drums. Berigan also played waltzes.

It was during their half that I was talking to a young lady who was next to where I sat when the full band played. (I normally sat on the left end in front, facing the dance floor.) She was attractive and alone. She said that her name was Catherine, and told me that she was a nurse taking care of an elderly man in the daytime. That night I took Catherine home and, as time went on, I kept seeing her. She would come to my room nightly and we started having an affair. She had explained to me that she had been married once and that she had had the marriage annulled after the first night. Her husband had been a brute, sexually. Catherine was a nervous girl when I met her and, when hearing a noise, or if I called to her, she would turn around quickly. But after our first affair she calmed down noticeably, and in a few days she was a calmer person.

On our first Sunday off we visited Pike's Peak, which is located about ninety miles south of Denver, near Colorado Springs. It was August, and a warm day when we left. When we reached

Colorado Springs we had lunch and then started the long climb up the peak. The road was steep and winding and we had to climb in low gear, bypassing the water tanks on the way up. Less than an hour later we reached the summit at 14,108 feet. It was snowing! We were dressed in summer clothes; I had on a sport shirt and Catherine a light summer dress. It was cold, and we went into the small coffee shop and ordered coffee to warm us. The air was thin and breathing was a little difficult. Our shivering soon stopped. There was no view because of the snow and clouds. We stayed about twenty minutes and then started back down the steep mountain, again bypassing the water tanks.

We soon reached Colorado Springs at the foot of the peak, and then we headed for Denver. We were nearing Denver when the car started to steam. I slowed down and came to a ranch, where some of the boys were staying. We waited an hour or so and I filled the radiator with cool water, foolishly not turning on the ignition. The engine block cracked. I had read somewhere that Ford was calling in all of the 1935 models and having the radiators changed free of charge. I crawled to the Ford repair shop and explained that the overheated radiator had caused the block to crack. They offered to change both free of charge. (This was conniving on my part.) We then took a cab to the hotel.

A few days later, at lunch time, I saw a sign in the window in a little coffee shop next to my hotel: "Lamb Chop Luncheon, 19 cents." I went in and tried it. The lone lamb chop, with whipped potato and vegetables, tasted good after a cup of soup. I finished off with dessert and coffee. "A bargain," I thought. Half an hour later I began to get cramps in my stomach and started throwing up. I put on my pyjamas and went to bed. Twenty minutes later I threw up again. I called the house physician and he came up. I told him what I had eaten and about throwing up. While talking to him I made a mad dash to the bathroom again. I came out and the doctor said, "Ptomaine poisoning." He gave me medication and told me to stay in bed and that I would be OK in a couple days. He left and I continued to retch every twenty minutes.

It was still early and I called Benny and told him I was ill and had to have a substitute that evening. He impatiently said, "OK." Back to the bathroom again and retched some more. I cursed that coffee shop. I called Catherine. She was obviously out at work. I just lay there and suffered the rest of the day and night. I could not retain the medication the doctor had given me, although I believe that he had also given me a shot.

The next day I was still feeling miserable but not retching as often. I called Catherine and told her the story. She said, "It's my day off, I'll be right over."

I said to myself, "Thank God, she's a nurse and can help me." Catherine soon arrived. I was pale and drawn, my bed was a terrible mess, and I was perspiring profusely. She gave me a sponge bath, made my bed, and put a damp cloth on my brow. Suddenly there was a knock on the door. Catherine opened it and who was there but Benny. Here I was the color of a sheet and with a cloth on my brow. I introduced Benny to Catherine, explaining that she was a nurse. Benny turned towards me, hardly acknowledging the introduction and said, "Art you look fine. I want you to come back to work tonight."

I replied, "I can't, Benny."

He said, "You have to, you'll be OK."

I reluctantly said, "OK." He left coldly without saying a word to Catherine. She stayed with me a while longer and then left.

Inconsiderate Benny, the best jazz clarinet player in the world!

Catherine had already bathed me, so all I had to do was to shave and dress, but it took me a long time to get ready. I hadn't eaten in two days and felt very weak. I wasn't even hungry. I staggered out the door and down to the lobby where I weighed myself. I had lost twelve pounds. I struggled through the job that night and went back to my hotel room, where Catherine was waiting for me. I felt a little better now. I slept much better that night, and in the morning I was able to eat a little breakfast. I went to work feeling a lot better the next night. At the end of the week Benny docked me a day's pay. Thoughtless Benny, the best jazz clarinet player in the world!

We played the last night in Denver and I went to my room, where Catherine was awaiting me. She helped me pack my bags, followed by a last romance. She cried softly. I didn't, but felt like it. I told her where she could write to me, and we parted, never to see each other again.

In the morning Allan Reuss and I got into my coupe and headed for California. I believe we went straight through to Oakland. We had a fairly good reception there, at the Sweets Ballroom, and then headed for Hollywood. Fortunately, we found a Spanish-style apartment on Berendo Street, a beautiful residential section lined with palm trees. It was near the Palomar Ballroom, where we were to play. Allan took an apartment for $14 per week and I chose one for $18.

Some of the cars were nicknamed. Harry Goodman and Gene Krupa drove together with all their equipment in back. This was called "The Death Car" after Harry had been side-swiped by another car at night and they were late for a one-nighter. Hymie Shertzer's car was called "The Corned Beef and Salami Car," for he and Pee Wee Erwin would make numerous stops along the way for those sandwiches. Red and Aggie Ballard, with Dick and Rhea Clark, also had a nickname for their car: it was called "The Silent Car," because they would drive hundreds of miles before anyone uttered a word. My car was named "The Racing Car," because we often drove it at a top speed of ninety miles per hour on the open road. We were always the first to arrive on the job. Of course Benny and Helen drove together in his Pontiac; we had no name for it, except that some of the boys derisively called it "The Old Man's Car."

FIVE

"Let's Dance"

We soon opened at the Palomar to a so-so crowd. People were curious to hear this new kind of band. Although they had heard us on the NBC show, people listened and danced with mixed emotions. The recordings that we had made in New York had begun to leak into the California music shops. The crowds grew nightly, and after two weeks the floor was jammed. Soon there was no room to dance, and people just listened. Benny was not a good mixer at that time and he was awed by the reception. His clarinet spoke for him, though; he was playing with great inspiration.

One unfortunate thing, however, was that Bunny Berigan was drinking heavily. He would play great until about 11 p.m., and after that he was impossible. Bunny was such a sweet man, it was a terrible shame. He had a pleasant personality, but was a loner; he preferred to drink and eat by himself while he was with the Goodman band. I would follow him around the golf course and invariably find an empty pint whiskey bottle in a sand trap. I did not drink at all in those days and felt sorry for this great artist. A little later Benny had to release him. However, his rendition of *I can't get started*, which he recorded later with his own band, goes down in history, in my opinion. I had also recorded with Bunny earlier—in 1933 with my brother Adrian. We recorded *Savage Serenade* and *Sweet Madness* on Perfect Records. Berigan and Goodman were both on that date and played extremely well.

Toots Mondello had not gone on the road trip. Hymie Shertzer was now playing first alto sax. Bill De Pew was on the other alto sax, and Dick Clark and I were on tenors. It was a good sax section! I had worked with Hymie long since when he was playing third alto. I taught him to open his throat on the high notes; before that he had the habit of pinching on the high notes. Now he was a full-fledged first alto man. Dick Clark and I shared the few tenor solos. Even at this stage Benny would look at Dick's bald head with disdain. He wanted a youthful looking band.

One night on the job Benny suddenly developed trouble with his clarinet. I was the nearest to him and he grabbed my clarinet, a Selmer like his, and inserted his mouthpiece and continued to play. He finished his solo and, while someone else was playing, he said, "Art, I'll give you fifty bucks and my clarinet for yours." I condescended, since I had little need for it, just playing a few clarinet backgrounds nightly. Benny reached into his pocket and threw a $50 bill on my stand. My clarinet was excellent (I had chosen it from many with the help of old man George Bundy, who was then president of Selmer), and later, in Chicago, Benny auctioned it off for a reputed sum of $1000. I repaired his clarinet easily.

There was comparatively little for the tenor men to really play, and most of our solos were in difficult keys. I had one in *Buddah Smiles* (in G♭ concert), and there were others in *Stomping at the Savoy* (D♭, *Remember* (A), and *Small Hotel* (D), but we hardly had a chance to warm up. So I saw four tenor men come and go on the other chair while I was with the band. A year later I became disenchanted too, but stayed with this great band anyway.

Benny knew I could play, because he must have heard my solos with Adrian, plus those on his own dates, but in this band I was terribly frustrated. I just satisfied myself with trying to improve the sax section. We seldom had to go over a new chart more than twice, even with Fletcher Henderson's difficult arrangements, which were always highly syncopated. Benny could read and transpose practically anything, and so could most of the other boys.

Benny and I played clarinet and tenor unison in octaves the following year on the first chorus of *Goodnight my Love* and we sounded like one man. The whole band thought and felt alike. This recording of *Goodnight my Love* featured sixteen-year-old Ella Fitzgerald on the vocal. After a hundred pressings it was discontinued because Ella was under contract with Chick Webb on Decca records. We later rerecorded it with Frances Hunt doing the vocal.

We were held over at the Palomar. The place was a madhouse

every night and the bar continued to do a tremendous business. When we finally finished at the Palomar we played one week at the Paramount Theatre in Los Angeles, then set out for Chicago. When we arrived in Chicago my 1935 Ford, in just seven months, had 17,000 miles on the odometer. It needed a brake and valve job plus tires. This was due to my high-speed driving: I would keep the accelerator down to the floor on the open roads and do eighty-eight to ninety miles per hour. (There were no speed limits on the open roads out west then.) I don't remember if we did any one-nighters on the way, but we opened at the Congress Hotel in Chicago on 6 November 1935.

Bunny Berigan and Benny had parted ways and the trumpet section now was composed of Harry Geller, a California boy, Ralph Muzzillo and Nate Kazebier. Pee Wee Erwin had been with us for some time. Joe Harris and Red Ballard were on trombones; Joe also sang well. We had the same sax section as in California. The rhythm section was also the same: Krupa on drums, Jess Stacy on piano, Harry Goodman on bass and Allan Reuss on guitar. Helen Ward was on vocals.

We opened with a good crowd. We had been called down to James C. Petrillo's office (he was Union Federation President) and he laid down a set of rules and regulations, one of which was, "If you go to another club and they ask you to take a bow, sit there, don't pay no attention. Look the other way if they put the light on you." It was obvious that he did not want us to exploit another club. He went on and on.

While we were at the Congress Hotel Tommy Dorsey phoned me backstage from New York. We exchanged greetings and he asked me to join his band. He could match my salary, but could not surpass it. I thought quickly and turned him down. I thought, why go to the number three band when I was already playing with the number one. Tommy pleaded, "Art, you are going stale in that band. Come with me and you can play as much as you want." I still turned him down.

We worked hard at the Congress. The boys were not netting much salary: together with the Chicago Union tax, social security (which had just been instituted) and withholding tax, our take-home pay was comparatively small. Mine was exceptionally small, since I was sending half my net salary to my mother.

Ena kept writing and becoming more impatient. She finally wrote me an ultimatum, saying that we get married or break up. I loved her and didn't want to lose her. So I wired her train fare to come out. I bought a platinum wedding ring and rented an apartment at the Lansing Apartments uptown: one room, kitchenette and bath for $18 per week. And I made arrangements at the church (High Episcopal, although I am Catholic).

She arrived on the morning of 25 November 1935 looking as beautiful as ever, and I was so happy to see her. We both cried. It had been so long. I had arranged for Allan Reuss to be our best man and we obtained our marriage license and were married in a simple ceremony in the priests' rectory. I was wet-eyed with happiness and she was in tears.

There was no honeymoon as I had to work that night. We set up housekeeping and had a bite to eat out, then went back to the apartment.

I invited her to the Congress Hotel for the evening, but she declined, saying that she didn't have adequate clothing to go to such a swank hotel. She was also very tired from the long train ride, so I bought her a bottle of champagne and a newspaper and she sipped champagne and listened to my little radio all evening by herself. She was a stoic girl, just nineteen years old, but afraid to step outside for a breath of air because it was a not-so-good neighborhood.

Right after work I rushed home in my car, which was new in age but old in abuse. I found Ena's eyes red from crying. She had listened to the broadcast from the hotel and heard me play, I believe, *Always*. We finished the bottle of champagne and went to bed. The next day I began to do some thinking. How were we going to make it? Here I had a widowed mother, a sick sister and now a wife. I wrote Adrian, who was still at the Tap Room, airmail. He broke the news to Mom, and she was not upset, thank God. I continued to send the same amount of money home, half of my net salary.

Ena kept a tight budget. She kept a little ledger and I gave her ten dollars a week for food. She would go out to the local market, buying day-by-day. After a few weeks Ena, who was normally 110 lbs and 5'3" tall, went down to 98 lbs. I went down to 135 lbs. I took her to a doctor whom the landlord had recommended. He gave her a thorough checkup and said she was OK. He suggested that she drink two bottles of beer a day, and charged me $2 for the visit. Beer was only twelve cents a bottle then, with two cents back on the return of the empty. Ena started to gain weight and was in better spirits now.

On Sunday December 8th we played at the Congress Hotel what may have been the first jazz concert in history.

Soon Benny got "The Elgin Watch Show" on radio in addition to the Congress Hotel job. Things were looking up, and I started sending considerably less than half my salary home each week. Ena regained her weight and so did I. We were eating well now, but she still didn't dare venture out at night, even to go to a movie. An aunt and uncle of mine finally located us and they would take Ena out a couple of nights a week. They would go bowling or to a bar.

One afternoon we went to the automobile show and liked the 1936 Olds Coupe. I knew that I would have to spend a lot of money repairing the Ford, so we went to an Oldsmobile dealer near our apartment. The Olds Coupe cost $826, even; there was no sales tax there. I asked, "What will you give me in trade for my Ford?" They looked it over. It was clean and shiny outside with no dents. The dealer said $525, and I had paid only $535 for it new! I said, "It's a deal," and we selected a baby-blue Olds Coupe.

The salesman, Mr McCullum, a middle-aged man and an alcoholic, said to me, "If you sell three cars to your band for me, I'll give you a free radio." He added, "I have the free parts at my disposal and have a man to install it." As a result, I sold seven oldsmobiles to the boys for him. He hemmed and hawed and finally gave me a radio.

Chris Griffin from CBS in New York joined the band while we were at the Congress and his wife Helen and Ena became fast friends. We finished the thirteen weeks on the "Elgin Show" almost simultaneously with our closing at the Congress. Things were looking up: we had originally been booked for one month and had stayed for six. Now we had a week off. Right after work Ena, Bill De Pew and I headed for New York in the Olds. Mind you, none of us had been to bed when we started the long trip, some 900 miles on the old roads. Neither Ena nor Bill drove, and while they slept I drove to Pittsburgh, where we dropped Bill off at his home. We continued on to Harrisburg, when I knew I could not take this punishment any longer. We checked into a hotel, slept four hours, and resumed our trip to New York. We arrived several hours later and were greeted cordially, Ena being accepted with open arms. After a five-day stay we headed back for Pittsburgh to pick up Bill De Pew, and returned to Chicago.

I always saved the itineraries for the coming month that our manager, Leonard Vannerson, distributed to us, naming the date, place of the engagement and a recommended hotel. Unfortunately they were all destroyed later in a fire at my home, so I do not know the exact sequence of dates. I do know, however, that at one point Ena, Allan and I drove after work from Toledo, Ohio, to Columbus, a distance of about 200 miles. It was very early and dawn was breaking. The birds were flying low and slowly due to the heavy air, and we were going fast. We plowed through flocks of birds who gained altitude very slowly. When we reached Columbus about four hours later I got out and looked at the grille of the car. There were four birds impaled, and we felt sad.

We continued our swing east, doing many one-nighters and finally playing New England. We played a college there and there was a huge turnout. I met my little friend Johnny Baker, a baritone sax man who was, I believe, a couple of years behind me in high school. He requested *Always*, which had been released on Victor records several months before. He and his friends gathered directly in front of me, their waists hardly reaching the level of the bandstand. After a four bar intro I had the first chorus, and played something entirely different from what was on our recording. After it was over Johnny Baker said to me, "What did you change it for?" Fans always expected solos to be played note for note as on the recording.

We played a series of one-nighters throughout the East and then worked our way west doing one-nighters and theatres. This time we went by train, having our own Pullman car. Leonard Vannerson arranged the details carefully. Benny had the drawing room, Helen Ward a compartment and the other boys had the berths. I always had a lower berth after having made a secret arrangement with Leonard. A few times Ena would come along and share the berth with me. It was a tight squeeze, but we made it. Sometimes we chartered a Greyhound bus when there were no rail connections.

In Salt Lake City, Utah, Benny called me aside between sets and whispered to me, "When we get to California, I'm going to get rid of that bald-headed son of a bitch," pointing to Dick Clark, the other tenor man. "Fickle Benny," I thought, "the best jazz clarinet player in the world!" Dick was a good player.

We arrived in Hollywood and Benny called a rehearsal. We were all stale from the constant traveling. I opened my sax case and pulled out my horn. The reed looked like a piece of corrugated cardboard. Momentarily, I had no lip. The bright spot of that rehearsal was the presence of a little thirteen-year-old red-headed girl by the name of Frances Gumm, who later became known as Judy Garland. She was truly a great song-bird, and had already reached her peak. We were very impressed. This was not the last time that I was to see Judy.

Ena and I rented an apartment with a Mrs Boyer, and a late model Plymouth Coupe. We reopened at the Palomar, and the crowds were extremely enthusiastic. I complained to Mrs Boyer about the sunlight which shone through our white window shades early in the morning. (We always retired late because of our late finish at the Palomar.) Mrs Boyer said, "Why don't you do what I do, put a black sock over your eyes and around your head, pinning it end to end." I tried it, and it worked.

Time went on and Dick Clark was leaving. Ena and I had gone to hear Gil Evans's band near the beach. Stan Kenton was playing piano and Vido Musso was on tenor. Vido impressed me. He had a huge tone. I told Benny and he said, "Send him down." I called Vido, who, incidentally, had had very little formal education, having come to this country from Italy at a very young age, and been shifted from one relative to another. He could read and write very little.

Vido came down to the Palomar and sat in on the last set. Benny didn't ask him to play any arrangements, but called out *Honeysuckle Rose*. Vido played thirteen choruses, each one more exciting than the previous one. Benny hired him.

Benny called me aside and said, "Tomorrow we are having a rehearsal at two o'clock. Will you go over the tenor books with

Vido at one o'clock?" I agreed. I met Vido the next afternoon at one and, with two tenors, we turned to the first number in the book, *Minnie the Moocher's Wedding Day.* Vido struggled. He couldn't read. We went over and over it, but with the highly syncopated charts he was lost. I said, "OK, Vido, let's go to the next number." I forget at the moment what it was, but it was the same struggle. Our one hour was over.

At two o'clock the band came in to rehearse. Vido struggled and Benny looked at me. I just stared back at him. Benny nodded his head knowingly. Vido sweated that night out and finally made his famous remark: "It's not the *notes* that bother me, it's them damn *restes!*"

That night he took the book home with him. The next night he did a little better, laying low on the parts that he was unsure of, and soon he did a creditable job at the bottom of the section with his big sound. He did a remarkable job on the solos, although his chord changes left something to be desired.

During July and August of 1936 we made a variety film, *The Big Broadcast of 1937.* Ray Milland was featured in this picture. I had a solo on *Bugle Call Rag,* for which they had to have a close-up. On close-ups they measure the distance between the camera lens and your body, and on this solo they measured from the camera to my nose which is the most prominent part. Everybody laughed! Vido nicknamed me "Shneeze."

We doubled at the Palomar and *Big Broadcast* for three weeks, having to rise at 5 a.m. to go to the studios after working a hard night at the Palomar (from 9 p.m. to 1 a.m.). We were all dead tired. When we got to the studio at seven o'clock we had to go to makeup and hair-cut check daily before shooting started at eight o'clock. We continued to double for three weeks, every man dead on his feet.

While at the Palomar a few of us went down to the Paradise Club in Los Angeles to hear Lionel Hampton's band. It was a good band and Benny had his clarinet with him and jammed with Hampton all night. I went home earlier. Later on Vido and I and the Goodman boys did a record date with Hampton: *Stomp* and *I'm confessing that I love you,* among others.

After we finished at the Palomar we headed east, and in September we went on "The Camel Caravan Show." We wound up at the Steel Pier in Atlantic City and did the "Camel Show" from there.

One afternoon Ena was listening to Alex Bartha's band on the lower floor. They were playing a show and Bartha was the house conductor. Ena was highly impressed with a trumpet player by the name of Ziggy Elman, who not only played great trumpet but also piano, baritone sax and vibes. She told Benny about this. He said, "Send him up." Ena did. At a "Camel" rehearsal Ziggy sat in on first trumpet and Benny hired him on the spot, paying off Sterling Bose, who had joined us in California. To this day Ziggy Elman had the most powerful sound that I have ever heard.

Martha Tilton was the vocalist now, Helen Ward and Benny having had a parting of the ways. Martha and Ena became fast friends and we went swimming in the ocean off the pier. On our first day at the beach I had bought a new top to go with my swim trunks. A top was a must then. The ocean was terribly rough that day and the girls stayed on the beach. I ventured into the water and the first wave (on which I usually glided) threw me onto the beach. My swim top was in shreds and I was bruised all over and that was the end of the ocean for that day.

In November we opened at the Manhattan Room in the Pennsylvania Hotel (now the Statler) in New York, the first of a series of engagements there. It was an exciting band and the crowds were excellent. We continued our "Camel Show," and in January 1937 Harry James joined. He had left Ben Pollack's band and arrived at the hotel with a beat-up old tuxedo. Benny promptly loaned him $22.50 for a new one at Howards. The trumpet section was more exciting now than ever. Harry James was a genius. He could read all of the highly syncopated charts at sight, and he played fantastic jazz solos—different every time. His father was a circus bandmaster, and I believe Harry had been able to play *The Carnival of Venice* at the tender age of twelve; he was certainly playing with big bands while he was still in short pants. He was also a good conductor and a fine arranger: he arranged *Peckin'* for Benny.

After the second set one evening I saw Benny in the men's room and I told him that I had jammed with Harry one night uptown after hours when we were at the Congress Hotel in

Chicago. He asked, "Why didn't you tell me that he was so great?"

I replied, "I just didn't want to see another man go."

The trumpet section now consisted of Harry James, Ziggy Elman and Chris Griffin, but the saxes and rhythm sections remained the same. The band was great. We all felt as one man. The saxes blended beautifully and the rhythm section was outstanding. At rehearsals we had no trouble with the charts: twice over and we had it, although they were often in difficult keys and highly syncopated.

I must differ with Bill Maher, the discographer of the Benny Goodman *Treasure Chest* of network performances taken from air-checks from the Penn Hotel. Bill claimed that Benny would use a different clarinet every evening. He did not. Bill interviewed me one afternoon in Roslyn, I believe around 1962, and borrowed one of my air-check recordings that we had made way back in 1934. He never returned it. It was a poor recording and, since we had gone on the air at 7 p.m. with no warm-up, the band was badly out of tune, but the recording had a great sentimental value to me.

Our picture, *The Big Broadcast of 1937*, had been released and our record sales were soaring. Benny had carte blanche at Victor records. If he liked a particular original by our arrangers, he would record it and become co-author. Our theme song, *Let's Dance*, taken from a Weber classic, *Invitation to the Dance*, was now famous throughout the world.

On February 6th we made a short-wave broadcast to Japan, where Goodman's records were receiving attention. The Japanese fans sent back a list of favorite songs, among them *Some of these Days*, *Sweet Sue*, *Dinah*, *Memphis Blues*, *Basin Street Blues*, and *Beale Street Blues*. It was plain to see that they were a little behind the times.

On February 13th, while we were playing the Pennsylvania Hotel, Ena and I were invited to Uncle Frank's house in Long Island City for our day off. We drove to Long Island City and found the house was dark. We rang the bell and the lights flashed on. They all shouted, "Surprise!" All the relatives were there, plus Hymie Shertzer, and I had a grand 25th-birthday party.

The party broke up at about 1 a.m. Adrian and Dixie asked for a ride to New York to their apartment on West 64th Street, and I drove crosstown with Ena at my side and Dixie on Adrian's lap. The lights were green. At Madison Avenue there was no light, but I assumed that it was supposed to be green and so continued to cross. A garbage truck coming from the north hit us broadside, plowing us into a light post. Instinctively I shielded Ena (who was pregnant) with my right arm and put my left hand up to my face. We were not hurt but the car was demolished. Fortunately, the pole kept us from turning over. I arrived at the Penn Hotel the next evening with two black eyes.

On 10 March 1937 the band gathered together at the Paramount Theatre for an early morning rehearsal and we found hundreds of kids milling about the theater. We opened that morning. Preceding this the kids were whistling and shouting during the showing of the Claudette Colbert film *Maid of Salem*. The band would come up on an elevator stage after a short organ recital by Jesse Crawford. The kids continued to scream and whistle as we ascended. We invariably opened with *Let's Dance* followed by Dean Kincaid's arrangement of *Bugle Call Rag*, in which I had a tenor sax solo after the clarinet and trombone breaks. The house was packed and the kids danced in the aisles screaming, whistling and shouting. We played *Bugle Call Rag*, *King Porter Stomp*, *Stardust* and others. The quartet, which now consisted of Goodman, Krupa, Teddy Wilson and Lionel Hampton, suddenly had the spotlight on them. They played *Tiger Rag* and *Body and Soul*.

Krupa's uniform was soaked with perspiration; Hampton was also perspiring profusely, his sweat dripping onto his vibraphone keys. The rest of the band was in a soft blue light and we could see the audience clearly. The girls would wave at us and many of the single boys in the band would motion to the girls to meet them at the stage door. After a show there would be many girls waiting at the stage door who would do anything to have a date with these boys. Fan mail poured in to each member of the band, giving telephone numbers, etc, but Benny stayed aloof. Gene Krupa, their idol, signed many autographs. I never saw him with a girl; he loved Ethel, his wife. The rest of us also signed hundreds, and I, for one, received a lot of fan mail that included propositions. I

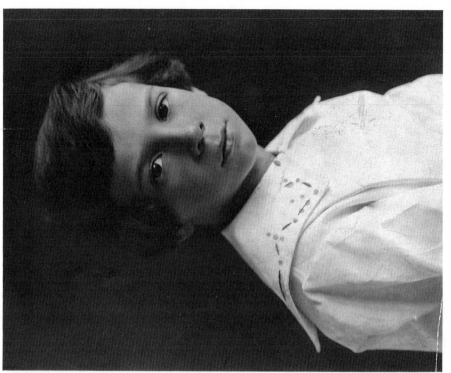

Adrian aged four and a half

Arthur aged four

Left: Baron Ferdinando Rollini

Right: Arthur aged eleven

Top: The house in Larchmont to which the family moved on 4 October 1917. Above: The special-bodied Ford (driver unknown) which Adrian sold to Paul Whiteman (see page 6)

Adrian's band, New Yorker Club, 1927: (left to right) Sylvester Ahola, Eddie Lang, Bill Rank, Chauncey Morehouse, Bix Beiderbecke, Adrian, Frank Trumbauer, Bobby Davis, Don Murray, Joe Venuti, Frank Signorelli

Adrian's band at Hunter Island Inn, 1931: (left to right) Carl Smith, Johnny Rude, Herb Weil, Arthur, Noel Kilgen, Adrian, Lew Coby, Chelsea Quealey, Bobby Davis, Jack Wechsler

Far Left: The Goodman band playing at a concert in Chicago, 1937: (bottom to top) Hymie Shertzer, Arthur, George Koenig, Allan Reuss, Jess Stacy. Left: Arthur returning to the USA from England in 1929. Below: Adrian in 1937.

Harry James, c1937

Ziggy Elman, c1936

kept many of these in my scrapbook. That opening day we had an attendance record of 21,000 people at the theater, mostly kids who had skipped school. The candy man sold approximately $900-worth of candy.

After the last show every evening we would hustle back to the Pennsylvania Hotel, where a relief band awaited us and we finished the evening. Pee Wee Monte was our band boy, and a good one. He was very energetic, and often did minor repair work on the instruments. We would always find our instruments ready to play. This man was incredible and we tipped him too little. (He had followed Bill Mather, a middle-aged Englishman who was freshly out of Adrian's Drum Shop; he found the going rough, perspiring profusely during the heat of summer.) Pee Wee was the man for the job. He would pack our instruments and we would find them all set up for us at the hotel.

Then on Thursday evenings, between shows, we would do the "Camel Show." We were terribly busy and I saw Ena very little during this time. I took a room at a hotel across the street for short naps between shows. I found it extremely difficult to get enough sleep during the night, although we lived on 90th Street.

The Paramount engagement was held over several weeks, thus holding back Eddie Duchin, the next scheduled band. After the Paramount and Pennsylvania Hotel engagements were over we hit the road once again. Before we left New York, however, we played a "Battle of the Bands" with Chick Webb at the Savoy Ballroom in Harlem. The critics called it a draw! We swung across the country on one-nighters, this time by train, and by chartered bus when we were unable to make train connections.

One time we played a one-nighter somewhere in the Middle West. The bus was packed after the job and we all piled in. We drew up to Benny's hotel and he walked in with a young lady. We were tired and kept waiting, one hour, an hour and a half. Finally Benny got into the bus with no apology. Inconsiderate Benny, the best jazz clarinet player in the world!

Another time we started out by chartered Greyhound bus, supposedly in a northerly direction. We drove and drove. I sat in front with Benny. I glanced at the road map. It was afternoon and the sun should have been to our left; instead, it was to our right. I said to Benny, "We're going in the wrong direction."

Benny said "You're crazy, Schneeze. The driver knows what he is doing." I glanced at the map again and showed him where there was a ferry, and the little town directly across the ferry had the dance hall where we were to play. Benny called to the driver, "Turn around!" Now the late sun was to our left. We had gone 150 miles out of our way.

Thereafter I navigated and at nightfall we arrived at the ferry. This was a barge type, with pull ropes. The boys hastily changed into their uniforms, disheveled and unshaven, and Pee Wee put the instruments on the float. The bus remained behind and we pulled ourselves across the small river. We helped Pee Wee carry the instruments into the dance hall across the river and unpacked and started *Let's Dance* at precisely 9 p.m., a very motley crew.

Benny never even thanked me. Thoughtless Benny, the best jazz clarinet player in the world!

We played the Chicagoan Theatre in Chicago. Most of the boys stayed at the Sherman Hotel. There was a huge blackboard in the lobby indicating your room number and time to be awakened in the morning. I knew Benny's room number and, after he retired, I would write down his number and time to be called. I would always write 6:30 a.m. after his room number. This blackboard later was placed near the telephone operator's desk. I was in the lobby one morning when Benny came down. I said, "Good morning, Benny how did you sleep?"

He replied, "Lousy. Some idiot keeps calling me at 6:30 in the morning!'

Later, while at the Penn, we had a recording session. The band was intact except for Walter Page, a black bassist from Basie's band, replacing Goodman's brother Harry. Another time it was a black guitarist, Freddie Green from the Basie band.

Just before the "Camel Show" one Thursday Leonard Vannerson came to me and said, "Art, I want to speak to you."

I said, "Leonard, we are going on the air in a minute and I have to adjust my music. Tell me after the show." After the show Leonard was gone. We had a recording session scheduled for the next morning. When I went down to the Victor recording studio for that session I found Lester Young sitting in my chair. I stayed in the small lobby outside. Benny came rushing out. Tears welled in my eyes. Benny said, "Don't worry, Schneeze, I am just trying something." I went home most unhappy.

The following night Benny invited me to his suite in the Penn Hotel and played *Tippy Tippy Tin*. He said, "What do you think?"

I said, "Frankly, Benny, Lester is a good man, but the balance stinks. Lester sticks out like a sore thumb." Inconsiderate Benny, the best jazz clarinet player in the world!

We headed for California again and arrived in Hollywood for the third time. Ena endured the whole tour, sleeping with me in the confines of a lower berth. We checked into Mrs Boyer's apartment house and rented a car. Ena was very much pregnant at this time. We contacted a Dr Moffit, an obstetrician who had been highly recommended, and we visited him. He was a kindly old gentleman who had great wisdom. He said to me, "It's too bad that most husbands cannot witness childbirth. It would give them a different outlook on the ordeal that a woman must face."

After a short time at the Palomar we started the film *Hollywood Hotel*, which required us to rise at 4 a.m. and go to the studios for makeup and hair-cut check. From there we were driven fifty miles in limousines to an airport. Most of us dozed on the way. Our opening scene in the film consisted of each of us with a chauffeur-driven Austin playing *Hooray for Hollywood*, the overture of which we had recorded in the studio the previous day. Jimmy Mundy, in order to garner double pay, arranged this in 2/4 time instead of the regular 4/4 cut time. This is unusual in jazz music, and posed a problem for Vido Musso. Benny and Jimmy Mundy wound up sharing the fourth sax chair. It was a spectacular scene during filming with all of those Austins converging upon the airport. We all had white suits, dark ties and white shoes.

Between takes at the airport we would play softball in a nearby field. Some of the boys, since it was also a private airfield, would ride planes between takes. One time the director called, "Places everybody," and no one was there except Benny and me. The rest of the boys were flying above the airport! The director asked, "Where in Hell are the men?"

I replied meekly, "Up there," pointing to the sky. When they came down the director promptly grounded us.

This same routine lasted for six weeks: Palomar, movie, and

"Camel Show." We were getting only three hours sleep or less per night. The boys were sleeping on tables and chairs between takes and several of them felt ill. One night, in desperation, I went to the bar and ordered a champagne cocktail, although I didn't drink at the time. It didn't help. We were all desperately tired.

Vido Musso was still the band clown. Vido would come out with expressions that were unbelievable. He would go into a drug store and say, "I have a headache, give me a Broomo," meaning Bromo Seltzer, or "Give me a dark sangwich," meaning one on rye bread. One day he said, "My brother-in-law had an accident."

I queried, "What happened, Vido?"

He said, "He was jacking up his car to change a flat tire when he was hit by another car."

I asked, "What happened then, Vido?"

He replied, "He had to have his leg cut out."

This went on and on. He would say, "Benny, play *Stumpin' at the Severe*" (*Stompin' at the Savoy*). At Christmas time he said, "I think that Benny is going to give us a president" (present). While in New York City, Vido, Ena and I passed the Empire State Building by car. Vido looked up and said, "Let's get the hell out of here before that thing falls on me." One time he was riding with me and we parked on a hill. I did not have my brakes set all the way, and the car started to roll back slowly. Vido looked out of the window and exclaimed, "Geeze, the oith's movin'." On another occasion he referred to a boat as having drowned when it sank.

I roomed with Vido for two days at one time and he asked if he could dictate a letter for me to write to his wife, Rose, because he couldn't write. I agreed and got a pad and pen. He dictated, "Dear Rose, How are you? I am fine. Love Vido." I addressed it and mailed it.

When he was in New York Vido would visit Otto Link, the sax mouthpiece expert, and try mouthpieces. You could hear his big tone up and down 48th Street, especially during the summertime when the windows were open. In later years, long after Goodman, I met him on Broadway. We exchanged greetings. I asked, "Vido, what are you doing now?"

He replied, "I'm going with Stan Kenton, he's going to pay me a good celery" (salary).

While riding in a cab to a "Camel" broadcast I turned to Vido and queried, "How's your wife?"

Vido gestured towards his groin and said, "She's having trouble with her . . .

I asked, "What do you mean, Vido?"

He answered, "You know, her, her . . . ovaltines" (ovaries). Another times we were in a hot dressing room during August and Vido blurted, "Open the windows, I'm gettin' sophisticated" (asphyxiated).

One night Vido came to work at the Pennsylvania Hotel with a huge boil on his neck. He was suffering all evening. The next night he was back with a bandage on it. I remarked to Vido, "How's your boil?"

He answered, "OK, I had it glantzed" (lanced). "The doctor put easy tape (adhesive tape) on it." So much of this.

Ena was ready to pop now. She spent most of her evenings with Chris Griffin's wife, Helen. We played a one-nighter in Fresno, California, and the place was jammed. Suddenly someone called me to the phone booth to receive a telegram. I closed the door, but people were yelling and screaming almost cutting off the sound. The voice said, "Helen had a baby girl. Everything is OK. Ena." Between sets I bought a box of cigars and distributed them among the boys the next day; 16 mm pictures were taken of this which I still have.

We went back to Hollywood after the engagement and I went straight to Hollywood Memorial Hospital, where I had previously made arrangements for Ena. No Ena. I found her at Helen Griffin's apartment, very much alive and still very much pregnant. I asked, "Where is the baby?"

She replied, "What baby?"

I said, impatiently now, "The baby that Helen spoke about in the wire."

She quickly said, "That was not our baby, it was Helen's." (Ena's sister-in-law was also called Helen.) I was completely exasperated, having given out all those cigars and having had a few drinks with the boys. A couple of days later, however, it was for real. Ena entered Hollywood Memorial Hospital and bore me a baby girl, whom we had pre-named Adrienne, after her talented uncle.

The band had now finished the film and the stint at the Palomar Ballroom almost simultaneously and we had to leave for New York the very next day. Reluctantly, I had to leave Ena and little Adrienne behind in the hospital. We received our checks for the film, which we promptly cashed. They were for a considerable amount of money, at least for a sideman. On the train on the way to New York most of the boys sat in our Pullman car, which at night was converted to a sleeper. Five of the boys went into the men's room and shot craps (dice). Vido was the big winner and when we got to Detroit he got off the train and said, "See yuz in New York, fellas." He went to a Buick automobile agency and paid cash for the best Buick that they had, a Roadmaster convertible, and was already in New York when we arrived.

We reopened at the Pennsylvania Hotel in a blaze of glory. One night I looked over to Vido's chair and he was gone. Babe Russin, a great tenor man, had replaced him. I do not know to this day what happened. Vido said no good-byes but just vanished. Babe was no match for Vido's strong tone but made up for it with his keen ear and great drive. He had just left CBS and was unaccustomed to our relaxed way of playing. He said to me, "You fellows lag."

I said, "Babe, that's our way."

He saw that he was no match in volume to the rest of the section and he said to me, "Art, can I borrow your mouthpiece to have the facing duplicated?"

I replied, "Sure, just bring it back to work tomorrow night."

He took the mouthpiece to Otto Link and had my facing put on his own. He came back to work that night with a bigger tone. The blend was still good. Babe was a good reader and read off all the charts at sight. On his second night on the job Babe said to me, "I see that Benny is still hogging it all" (meaning the reed solos).

One night Babe came to work and said to Benny, "I saw you at Fifth Avenue and 58th Street today."

Benny asked, "What was I doing?"

Babe answered, "Picking your nose!"

Benny at this time became more and more critical. He would listen to each solo intently. I would get solos written on my sheet but, seeing so many men come and go, I began to hand them over, first to Vido and then to Babe. I was content with playing what I had, and said to myself, "Let the other guy try to please Benny."

It was 1938. On January 16th we played the first jazz concert ever in Carnegie Hall. The place was filled to capacity. Harry James was the first one to come on stage. He remarked to the man behind him, "I feel like a whore in church." Our initial feeling of awe soon vanished and we settled down to our usual performance. Benny was elegant in full dress and the boys of course wore tuxedos. I had a brief sixteen-bar solo in *Blue Skies*. Babe had solos in *Don't be that way* and *Sing, sing, sing*. Jess Stacy played magnificently on *Sing, sing, sing*. Vernon Brown had replaced Murray McEachern shortly before and also had a solo on *Don't be that way*. (Murray later went with Whiteman, where he was featured on trombone and alto sax. He was a great talent but Benny seldom let him play.)

The acoustics at Carnegie Hall were the best that I had ever encountered. You could hear yourself and each individual in the band with ease. Later Benny made the band play pianissimo, and this was difficult for some men. Helen Ward's husband, Albert Schwartz, had attached a second mike to the house mike and was recording backstage. We were relieved by a black group made up of Count Basie, Lester Young, Buck Clayton and other jazz greats, plus Duke Ellington stars Cootie Williams, Johnny Hodges and Harry Carney. Bobby Hackett was a guest also. Martha Tilton sang *Loch Lomond*.

Carnegie Hall was a great success and I had the pleasure of recording there several times after that with other orchestras, some as large as fifty men.

We opened at the Paramount Theatre again. Mae West was in the film *Every Day's a Holiday*. Once again, most of the kids would be there between five and seven o'clock in the morning, some even bringing their lunch along. They would light bonfires to keep warm in the winter cold. They didn't have to worry this time about skipping school, because they were between semesters; exams were over and they were more exuberant than ever. The police had to keep them in check.

After several weeks at the Paramount we swung into a theater tour. Benny became more critical with his men. He would listen to the notes of each man's solos intently, which made most of the men very uncomfortable and nervous. We arrived at the Earle Theatre in Philadelphia and Benny became critical of Gene Krupa. When Benny stared at a man we would call it "the Paralysis Ray," later shortening it to "the Ray." He was giving Gene's bass drum "the Ray." This went on for a few days and Gene couldn't stand it any longer. Finally, on stage, in full hearing range of all of us, Gene (who rarely swore) flared up and blurted, "Eat some shit, Pops!" After the show he went to his dressing room and tore up his high-priced contract and finished the week. Gene's parting remark to me was, "If you get hot feet, Schneeze, come with me. I'm forming my own band."

Meanwhile Benny had Lionel Hampton play drums until he found a replacement for Gene. Lionel was a good drummer and would add a little comedy to the show by throwing his sticks high in the air and catching them, and he also did a back-scratching scene with his sticks. He was incredible.

Gladys Hampton, who owned several fur coats, was very frugal with Lionel. He would have to beg her for money. I was with him one day on the train when he asked Gladys for a dollar. She replied, "Where is the fifty cents I gave you yesterday?" Lionel pleaded and she finally condescended to give him a dollar. He said, "Art, let's go back to the club car for a beer." I walked back with him and we sat down. I said, "Dutch treat, Lionel." Each of us ordered a bottle of beer and the steward obliged. We drank our beer slowly and then asked for our checks. The steward brought two checks, each of them for forty cents, which was a little high for that time. Lionel gave him the dollar and said, "Keep the change." His dollar was shot. I paid for my beer and tipped the steward less generously.

On our last visit to the Fox Theatre in Detroit Lionel had no money. Between shows for those two weeks he ran up a tab of $62.50 at a local bar. On our day of departure Gladys was presented with the bill and she beat Lionel unmercifully with a wet towel, so the wives said. Gladys is no longer with us, so I may tell this story.

We played the Lyric Theatre in Indianapolis and then the Fox in Detroit, where I became ill with strep throat and had a temperature of 104 degrees. I called the house doctor and he came up and administered a drug which cut the fever, but I had a terrible pain in my throat, and couldn't even think of eating. That day Benny had a substitute for me: Bus Bassey, a good tenor man, but a prankster, from Detroit. I was still suffering the next day when I heard a knock at the door. I opened it and who was there but Ena. Her intuition had told her that something was wrong and she left little Adrienne with my mother and took the first train out. She had first gone to the theater looking for me, and Martha Tilton, who had been waiting to go on stage, told her that I was ill at the hotel. Ena rushed right over and found me in that condition. I missed two days of work. On the second day Bus Bassey was in my chair again. Benny, apparently near-sighted, said to him, "How do you feel, Schneeze?" The boys laughed. The only similarity between us was that we both wore a small mustache. I took Bassey's telephone number and kept it in my wallet, because I had ideas for the future.

Allan Reuss, my buddy and best man, had long since left, and George Rose joined on guitar at the Fox Theater. Benny auditioned George in his dressing room, seemed to be impressed and signed him to a contract. The first week George was in front of the band, the second week next to the saxes, the third week next to the brass, the fourth week next to the drums and the next week, out. He took his contract to the Detroit union local. They examined it and found no signature for Benny Goodman; there was only a space for the signature and his name typed in. George was out. Fickle Benny. George was a funny man who did a great imitation of Frankenstein.

We went back to the Pennsylvania Hotel. One night I looked over to the fourth sax chair and Babe Russin had vanished. Bud Freeman was playing in his chair and I still don't know what happened. Benny hired Buddy Schutz from Vincent Lopez's band to play drums. He signed him up to a year's contract and then, after two weeks, didn't like him. Lionel was put back on drums and Buddy Schutz, to honor his contract, would come to work nightly and sit behind the curtain in back of the bandstand.

Lionel was a great drummer but was only filling in temporarily until Davey Tough completed his two-week notice with Tommy Dorsey. One night he must have been drinking and was a little high. We played a ballad. It got slower and slower and by the third chorus he was laboring. If it had gone only one more chorus, the band would have come to a complete halt.

Soon Davey Tough joined us, all 115 lbs of him. He was a fine drummer but heavy on the cymbals. Benny eyed him cautiously. Meanwhile, Buddy Schutz was still lounging comfortably behind the rear curtain. He was always on time and sat and sat through the whole evening, smoking cigars. The pressure began to take a toll on little, slender Davey. He was losing weight. Benny was very critical with drummers.

After making his final recordings with Goodman on the 23rd of December Harry James left the band at the end of the month. In our Pullman car Benny mentioned that Harry was a machine. After Harry left he called me to do his first recording session with him, and I had a solo on *Lullaby in Rhythm*. With his own band he went a little commercial, recording such songs as *You made me love you*, and others. He found this to be more lucrative.

Hymie Shertzer left the band to go with Tommy Dorsey. Milt Yaner came in on first alto for a week or two and then Benny traded him to Jimmy Dorsey for Noni Bernardi. George Koenig had long since gone because Benny had accused him unjustly of lighting one of those trick matches that create snow flakes. George, who had been with the band on third alto for a long time, was fired. Dave Matthews, Harry James's friend, was on third alto and Bud Freeman on the other tenor chair.

The section was falling apart. Bud, a great player who had previously been with Tommy Dorsey and played some great solos with that band, told me years later that I was the only one who could read in that sax section. This was not true. I saw that Bud's tenor was badly out of tune and recommended the make that I had. He sounded much better with the new horn. When Bud first joined the band, on solos Benny would say, "Take another one, Bud," then another and another. Bud blew his brains out. Finally after three weeks, Benny, as fickle as he was, would turn the other way and whistle while Bud played his now meager solos. Maybe it was Bud's bald head that got to him, who knows?

Benny Heller, a solid rhythm guitar player from Alex Bartha's Steel Pier band in Atlantic City, was called in. He had a strong sound and good time, and stayed for my duration.

While Bud Freeman was with us we played a date in Salem,

Massachusetts. The hall was crowded and we did not venture far off the bandstand. Joe Dixon's father was behind the curtain with a gallon of Italian red wine which he had made. Bud and I started off drinking Coca-cola from bottles with a straw. We passed the empty bottles back to Mr Dixon and he would refill them with wine. We continued to sip. Benny obviously thought that we were drinking Coke. Bud and I remained on the stand all evening, sipping and sipping. We were both feeling no pain, and we continued to get refills. The wine was cool and the evening very warm. I was unaccustomed to drinking, and felt very drunk. Still we sipped on. At the end of the night I could hardly get off the bandstand. Pee Wee packed my horns and I got off the stage somehow.

There was a dense fog that night, and I carefully made my way to the chartered bus that was waiting to take us to Boston for a theater engagement. The bus driver threaded his way through the fog, and much later we arrived safely in Boston. The fog was so dense that I had to feel my way to the front door of the hotel. Ena, now driving, was to meet me there, leaving little Adrienne with my mother. I entered my room and felt ill, and headed straight for the bathroom. Ena was asleep and I did not want to disturb her. I bent to the floor on my knees and retched into the bowl. Ena awakened at the sound and came in, giving me comfort, and was not even angry, just sympathetic. I went to bed, and awakened in the morning with the worst hangover in history! We opened the next day at the Keith Memorial Theatre and I had a head like a balloon. I vowed then and there that I would never drink again. I partially kept my promise.

One night in particular the band sounded badly. Noni Bernardi was on first sax, Dave Matthews on third sax, and Bud Freeman and I on tenors. Benny was impatient, eyeing each man and gently stomping his foot. After a set Noni Bernardi, who was raised by priests and was highly religious, called me aside. He said, "This man is Goodman, but he is a badman." The band actually did sound bad, however, and this time Benny was right.

Martha Tilton was replaced by Louise Tobin, Harry James's beautiful former wife. Louise sang well, but just a shade under pitch. Leonard Vannerson was sad at having lost Martha. Buddy Schutz was still in back of the bandstand every night and, on one-nighters when Benny left before the last set, Buddy would sit in, just to keep in shape. Davey Tough was now down to a mere 95 lbs. On a one-nighter four of us sat down to dinner before going to work but Davey was completely exhausted. He said to the waitress, "Bring me a cup of black coffee so I can stay awake for the meal." We laughed. He was skinny as a rail with the pressure. In July he left and was replaced by Nick Fatool, a solid drummer.

In January 1939, for reasons still unknown to me, I was voted into the *Metronome* magazine's "Best All Around Tenor Sax" column and recorded on Victor with the All Star band. We recorded two sides: *Blue Lou* and *The Blues*, a head arrangement. The men included Benny Goodman, Hymie Shertzer, Bunny Berigan (Bunny was sober), Jack Teagarden, Tommy Dorsey, Harry James, and Eddie Miller on the other tenor. (He took the solo on *Blue Lou* and I took the one on *The Blues*.) Bob Zurke was on piano, Ray Bauduc on drums, Bobby Haggart on bass and Carmen Mastren on guitar. Sonny Dunham and Charlie Spivak were on the other trumpets. During *Blue Lou* Benny took Hymie off to the side and played first sax himself; Hymie played third.

One night, a little before this time, when I looked over at the fourth sax chair, Bud Freeman had mysteriously disappeared and Jerry Jerome, a fine player from the Red Norvo band, was playing the other tenor. He was the fifth man to fill that chair since I had been with the band. Altogether I had seen some eighty men come and go, perhaps more. I must state emphatically, though, that the 1937–8 band was the best! Apart from Hymie Shertzer, who could swing a great lead alto sax, this band consisted entirely of jazz soloists of great talent. Unfortunately, however, they did not get a chance to exhibit their talents, as Benny preferred to do most of the solo work himself.

Anyway, Artie Shaw was now voted the number one band in the country, and we were number two. After this Benny practiced high notes tirelessly in his dressing room for several days.

Benny fired his brother Harry (or maybe Harry quit, I do not know), and he was replaced by Artie Bernstein, a great bassist who at that time would consume large quantities of alcohol without batting an eye.

It was sometime in April 1939 that we received our monthly itinerary and I saw that we were to be in New York one month later. Very shortly after that, in the Fox Theater in Detroit, I was practicing alone in my dressing room. I wanted to give Benny my notice, but he had already left the theater, as had everyone else except Leonard Vannerson, who was in his dressing room a flight below mine. I heard footsteps shuffling up the stairs and assumed it was Leonard. As he neared the top of the stairs I called out, "Leonard!" The voice said, "Yes." By now he was entering my room. I said, "Leonard, I want to leave the band when we get to New York next month. I'm tired of the road and the band is not the same." Whether or not he was coming up to get rid of me, I'll never know because he's dead now. I gave him Bus Bassey's telephone number. The headlines in *Down Beat* read, "Rollini included in Goodman purge." Ena was angry.

We had had a softball team with the band earlier. We defeated the teams of all the other bands, including Count Basie's, during which game Lester Young hit a ball far over my head in left field for an inside the park home run. Harry James was our best pitcher. Vernon Brown played first base and was a good long-ball hitter. Lionel Hampton was the catcher and another long-ball hitter. Noni Bernardi, who had played semi-pro ball, was on third base, Red Ballard played second base or shortstop, Chris Griffin played center field and Dave Matthews right field. We used to call Dave "Twinkle Toes" because of his unusual step. The other positions varied. We had our own softball uniforms and equipment.

One day in Toronto, Canada, we played a double header, winning both games against a Canadian band. I was sore all over after that one and spent all afternoon the next day in a hot bath. We were still undefeated. Then Bud Freeman booked a game at the University of Rochester, where we were to play a one-nighter, but these men were intercollegiate champions and they made monkeys out of us. Red Ballard, first up, struck out. I bunted and was thrown out. The ball kept coming in like a bullet and we were helpless. They started to bat from the opposite side in mockery and defeated us 16 to 9. That was the end of our previously undefeated team.

My one month's notice was half up, when we played a one-nighter in Minneapolis. I made the acquaintance of two girls on the sidelines and they asked me where we were going next. I innocently told them we were headed for a theater in St Louis, where we were to play for a week. We took the train that night to St Louis and checked into a hotel in the morning. Ena had driven to St Louis with Aggie Ballard in our new La Salle (a small Cadillac), and she checked in with me.

The following morning, while we were still sleeping, the phone rang. Ena groggily answered it and then turned it over to me. My God, it was one of those females that had followed us from Minneapolis! This girl certainly had nerve and said that she would see me at the theater. I said, "No!" I hung up the phone.

Ena, only partially awake, asked, "Who was that?"

I replied, "Some twelve-year-old kid who wants lessons." She was satisfied and went back to sleep.

I got to the theater and next-door there was a luncheonette. These girls came out and invited me in. One of them was calling to an imaginary dog. These girls were far out. I was glad to get out of St Louis.

Ena and Aggie left for the theater in Cleveland, our last stop before reaching New York. The wives would congregate in Louise Tobin's dressing room at the theater and stay all day. Louise was very beautiful and had a figure such as that of Daisy Mae in the "Li'l Abner" comic strip, except that she was a brunette. She would often change in front of the girls, and Ena told me that she had a beautiful body.

The week in Cleveland seemed very long, because I was anxious to get home to New York. The band was falling apart and Benny's back (he had slipped a disc) was bothering him. "The Camel Show" was scheduled to go off the air in a little over three weeks and I was tired. So were the other men.

We reached New York and Ena and I took a few days off in Salt Point, my mother's summer place. I tuned in to the last "Camel" broadcast; Toots Mondello was playing first alto and Bassey had replaced me. I felt sad because I had been with this great band for five years and had seen it rise and fall. Soon after, Ena and I went to the Waldorf Astoria to hear the band. There had been several changes and it still sounded good, though not sensational. Benny's back was bothering him more and he soon broke up the band to have an operation. Some of the men went on the West

Coast with Artie Shaw; he was now number one, with Glenn Miller fast rising to the top.

An interesting thing about Benny, he would go through a box of clarinet reeds in five or ten minutes. He would wet a reed and, without putting on the ligature, would blow a couple of notes and throw the reed to the floor. He would find maybe one or two good reeds that suited him out of a box of twenty. Pee Wee Monte would pick them up and carefully put them in boxes for me. I arrived home with ten boxes of clarinet reeds. Benny would say, "I wish those Frogs (meaning Frenchmen) would send me some good reeds."

Benny and I parted good friends. Later, while I was at NBC, Benny called me for a Disney soundtrack and, during the war, for a V-disc. He also called me for a southern tour, which I couldn't make, and even called me in the 1960s for an engagement at Freedom Land in the Bronx, which I also couldn't make.

In 1978, after hearing the 40th-anniversary tape of the 1938 Carnegie Hall concert, Jack Sheldon reminded me of an incident that happened after a one-nighter in Pennsylvania. I had been sitting next to Benny in a diner when he ordered scrambled eggs. This was put before him and he promptly took the ketchup bottle, with its top on, and shook it over his eggs. The cap fell off in the middle of his dish. Instead of removing it, he ate all around it, leaving the cap and a little island of egg under it. Absent-minded Benny, the best jazz clarinet player in the world!

Another incident occurred while we were playing a one-nighter in Nuttings on the Charles. The hall was located on piles over the Charles River in Massachusetts. It was a hot night and the place was jammed full with no room to dance. As we played everyone stomped to the beat and the place shook with this terrible vibration. The manager squeezed through and stopped the band, fearing a collapse of the building. The police were called in and they evacuated eight hundred people from the vast crowd.

In later years, when Helen Forrest was the vocalist, Benny and Helen were going to a record date and Benny hailed a cab. The cab pulled up and Benny and Helen entered and started chatting. They hadn't left the curb when the driver turned around for directions. Benny put his hand in his pocket and asked, "How much do I owe you?" Absent-minded Benny, the best jazz clarinet player in the world!

After leaving Goodman I did a week with Richard Himber and a week with Van Alexander at Loews State Theatre, practically across from the Paramount. It was a large orchestra of about eighteen men, including strings, and I wisely took the names and telephone numbers of all the musicians. At the end of the week I went up to Don Albert's office for my check. George Stoll was there. He had been Bing Crosby's conductor for a long time and I knew him from Hollywood. He said, "Hello, Art. You are just the man I want to see. I need a band right away for the Capitol Theatre. We are opening on stage with Mickey Rooney and Judy Garland, and *The Wizard of Oz* is the featured film. Can you help me?"

I replied, "Of course." Using most of the men with whom I had played at Loew's State, plus a few additions, I had a band assembled in two evenings.

SIX

No pressure at all

I believe that we had two rehearsals before opening. Unlike when I was playing with Goodman, we got paid for these. I was both player and contractor. Between shows we kept busy. We jammed a couple of times with Georgie Stoll, who played jazz violin. I would take my clarinet to his dressing room and, with a guitar for rhythm, we played *Tea for Two* and many other tunes.

Mickey Rooney did not venture out into the street during intermissions; he would have been mobbed if he had set foot outside the theater. He was only eighteen years old and had just come off the "Hardy" series with Judy Garland. I was talking to Mickey after the first show on the second day. He paced back and forth like a caged tiger. I said, "Mickey, do you play ping-pong?"

He replied, excitedly, "Yes."

I said, "Suppose I send for a table and we'll split the cost?"

He said, "OK." I called Macy's department store and ordered a table, four paddles, a net, and a dozen balls. They arrived later that day and we had the table installed in the downstairs lounge backstage. I had thought that I was a good player, having won the hotel championship at the Shelbourne Hotel in London some ten years earlier, but I had played very little up to this time. Well, try as I did, Mickey (who was a fine athlete) would invariably beat me, usually 21 to 18. I think I beat him only twice the whole time that we were there. This kid was fantastic.

The show continued for three weeks and featured young Judy, a pretty girl just about sixteen years of age, who sang brilliantly. I do not remember the exact routine of the show, but I do know that Judy and Mickey did some skits. (I also did a few Studebaker transcriptions at night with Himber during this period, and a morning record date.)

On the last day and before the third show, George Stoll, our conductor, asked me if I knew of a good restaurant at which we could have a dinner party for the cast. He said that he would treat. I immediately thought of the Piccadilly Hotel where Adrian was playing with his trio, and made reservations for the whole cast there. We sat at one long table. Judy was there but Mickey was not; people peered between the heavily draped windows for a glimpse of Judy, and soon the sidewalk was crowded. Adrian's trio sounded superb, although he had gone commercial for monetary reasons. We finished our splendid dinner and George Stoll asked Adrian for a blank check. Adrian obliged and George paid the tab.

When we got back to the Capitol Theatre just before the last show, I asked Mickey, "What do we do with the ping-pong table?"

Mickey answered, "Take it home."

We had built a home on Long Island and the table fit perfectly in our large playroom, where we had a bar, laundry room, coat room and movie projection room with a real movie screen which I had obtained from my next-door neighbor Sid Kramer, a film distributor for RKO. Mickey and Judy had also given me their autographed pictures, which I hung on the wall.

I knew that Richard Himber was looking for a tenor man. Johnny Sedola was leaving, so I called him and he asked me to join the band at the Pierre Hotel, a swank hotel on Central Park South. I agreed. The money was poor, but I desperately wanted to stay in New York and did not want to travel any more.

Lou Shoobie, the contractor for CBS, had called me at 90th Street during my last year with Goodman and offered me a studio job. I turned him down because I thought studio bands were stiff and corny at that time. Today on TV the staff bands are excellent.

I opened with Himber at the Pierre Hotel, where we had eighteen men, including strings. Hank D'Amico was playing third sax and jazz clarinet. He was one man who did not try to imitate Goodman. He had a distinctive style of his own, and, as they now say, ears. He could read and transpose almost anything. However, he played poor alto sax. His only problem was that he was an alcoholic and would keep a bottle of whiskey in his locker downstairs in the bandroom. Hank had a seven-year contract with Himber and it still had about six and a half years to go. He would get bombed nightly and, in desperation, Himber hired another man to sit along side of Hank to play when he was loaded.

I opened the broadcasts playing the theme song on tenor sax. I also had a lot of jazz work this time—not eight or sixteen bars, but choruses. Although the money was not as good as with Goodman or at the Capitol Theatre, I felt relaxed and played with abandon. We did several Studebaker transcriptions and recordings as well.

Finally New Year's Eve 1940 rolled around. Himber was a non-drinker and non-smoker and before we started to play he said, "I don't want anyone to drink. I will have champagne for the whole band at midnight." Well, this edict was obviously directed at Hank, mainly because the other men drank very little. Hank actually stayed sober and Himber timed the sets so that we would finish one at five minutes to midnight. After playing *Auld Lang Syne* we all took our places at a long table. Three waiters came out with eighteen champagne glasses and three bottles of domestic champagne. They poured down the line but the glasses were steadily decreasing in content. Hank D'Amico was sitting at the end of the table and when the waiters got to him there were only about five drops of champagne left for his glass. We all laughed and so did Hank. He promptly got up from the table and went down to his locker and got terribly loaded. The other man had to finish for him, for we worked until three o'clock that morning.

Hank continued to drink and finally Himber went to the union and had his contract voided because of drunkenness on the job. Joe Viola then joined the band on third alto and clarinet. Joe was a schooled clarinet player and an excellent sax man. We continued at the Pierre and did Studebaker transcriptions and record dates during the day.

Himber was an uncouth person, to say the least. He would eat a diet of health foods and with his back to the band, baton facing the audience, he would pass wind silently and a few seconds later turn his head around to see the reaction. Then he would chuckle with his crooked smile. This went on almost nightly.

There was absolutely no pressure with this band except for payday. One such day I went to Himber's suite upstairs for my pay check. His beautiful secretary was behind her desk. I sat opposite her in a chair and she was just handing me my check when Himber entered one door of the suite, passed us, passed wind loudly, and marched out the opposite door. That was his idea of fun. My checks never included the exact change. If the check was supposed to be for X number of dollars and 76 cents, he would never include the change—just a flat sum of dollars. He was able to pocket about ten or twelve dollars a week this way.

After a long stay at the Pierre Himber announced that we were going on the road. I said to myself, "No, not again." I asked him, "Any one-nighters?"

He said, "No, we are going to Sam Maceo's place in Galveston, Texas, for three weeks." This was a gambling place. I thought that this would be a good opportunity for a vacation, so Ena, Adrienne and I packed the car and headed southwest, together with a Canadian vocalist and his blond wife. They were broke and Himber had advanced them a little money. This couple in the back seat bickered constantly.

We reached West Virginia and noticed a small wisp of smoke coming out of the roof vents of a huge mansion. I stopped the car and went to investigate but found no one there. I searched all around, and meanwhile the smoke was getting thicker. I finally walked into the woods and found a cabin and the caretaker. I told him about the smoke and he went to investigate. He explained that the owners of this mansion, also owners of the Lauree Caverns, were on vacation in Florida. He went back to his cabin and called the nearest fire department, some thirty miles distant. Small flames were now erupting from the roof. As we watched, the roof was soon ablaze and we were helpless. A half hour later two fire trucks arrived and started to pour water on the roof, but the flames were now shooting out of the second-story windows and the fire truck water tanks were quickly emptied. They hooked into the open well but that too soon ran dry. Inside of three hours we stood by helplessly and watched a beautiful mansion burn to the ground. When there were just embers little Adrienne picked up a stick and started towards the fire. I demanded, "Where are you going?"

She replied, "I just want to put a stick on the fire."

We resumed our ride to Galveston amid the continued bickerings of the vocalist and his wife. When we reached Galveston I was delighted to get rid of them. Fortunately, they took an apartment elsewhere.

We opened at Sam Maceo's. The drinking water in Galveston was terrible with a strong taste of sulphur; not even ice could kill the taste. On the job the boys would sip gin and Seven-up in the bandroom. Himber would check the bandroom regularly and ask, "What are you drinking?"

We all chorused, "Seven-up."

During the afternoons we would congregate on the beach: Godfrey Hirsch (drums), Gene Traxler, Milt Schatz (first alto) —we called Milt "Ma Schatz" because he was the band "mother" —Joe Viola, Lester Merkin, Hy Small and Jesse Ralph, and we also had a harpist, whose name slips me now. Eddie Stone was our pianist.

My cousin Phil Sillman, a fine drummer, also visited; he had been playing with George Hall nearby while on tour. At the end of the three weeks, I had a deep tan, deeper than ever before.

Next we were off to play at the Roosevelt Hotel in New Orleans during Mardi Gras season. The town was a bedlam. Then after three weeks we headed for Baton Rouge for two days. We fished at Lake Ponchartrain, catching a nice mess of fish. Then it was home to New York, happily without the bickering vocalist and his wife.

Himber then booked a three-week engagement at a gambling casino in Covington, Kentucky, across the Ohio River from Cincinnati. The river was swollen, due to the heavy rains for many days before we arrived. We checked into the Cincinnatian Hotel, the flood waters up to street level. Yank Lawson, who had been with Himber's band previously after leaving Bob Crosby, was playing jazz trumpet, and Ralph Muzzillo, formerly a bandmate while I was with Benny Goodman and now with an extremely strong sound and drive, was on first trumpet. Yank (who many years later became co-leader with Bob Haggart of the World's Greatest Jazz Band with such sidemen as Billy Butterfield, Bud Freeman and Bob Wilber) had a few too many drinks one night. After the job he went upstairs to the crap tables and made nineteen straight passes, and with side-betting against himself came away winning only $100.

Before going to work at night we usually ate at the hotel coffee shop. Ralph Muzzillo approached Himber, who had been sitting in a booth with some people, and asked him for a ten-dollar loan until payday. Himber reached into his pocket and handed Ralph a twenty-dollar bill, requesting change. Ralph got change of the bill and handed Himber the ten dollars change. Himber absent-mindedly put the money in his pocket and continued talking to the people. On payday Himber deducted twenty dollars from Ralph's salary. Ralph became infuriated when he couldn't reason with him. So on our closing night, after the job (when all the music books had been packed in their black fiber case), Ralph quietly opened the case and took out the first trumpet book, which he put under his coat. He got in the cab and headed back to our hotel across the Ohio River Bridge. Half-way across the bridge he stopped the cab, got out and threw the book into the river, and continued on to the hotel. Once back in New York, Himber found that his first trumpet book was missing. His library was insured for $5000, and in two days he had new first trumpet parts copied from the scores. He came out ahead of the game!

Himber soon announced that we were going to Chicago. He made a few changes in the band because some of the men wanted to stay in New York. He made a change in the string section, picking up three kids just out of the Juilliard School of Music and led by Arnold Eidus, a young, promising violinist who played a Stradivarius, which was given to him by a wealthy society woman. The kids were green, however, not having had any dance-band experience.

In Chicago we checked into the Sherlore Apartments and opened at the Edgewater Beach Hotel. We did well there with good airtime and good charts. I had a lot to play in the band, a solo in practically every number. I felt free—no "Ray" watching me or the other men. We stayed there three weeks.

Finally we were in our last week and Himber called five of us to one side and said, "I'm taking five of you to California and sending the rest of the band back to New York." We finished out the week, Himber passing wind as usual and turning his head around for the usual reaction. He bought upper-berth tickets for the band members that he was sending home, making them get up at 6 a.m. at Altoona, Pennsylvania, and move into a coach car for the remainder of the trip. He wired ahead to a California contractor for the additional needed men. The five he started with were Artie Friedman, first alto, Joe Viola, third alto and jazz clarinet, Dick Judge, vocalist, Eddie Stone on piano, and myself on tenor. Himber again gave me the train fare for car expenses and Ena, Adrienne and I drove to California while the others took the train. Ena now drove and was able to alternate with me; one of us would drive while the other slept. We stopped just long enough to check into a motel, shower, take a nap and change clothes, and then resumed our trip. We didn't drive any faster than seventy or seventy-five miles per hour tops on the open roads.

We got to Hollywood in late January 1941, and did some Studebaker transcriptions with different guests each show, Dorothy Lamour being one. Himber announced, "We are opening at the St Francis Hotel in San Francisco January 30th."

I said, "Give me my car transportation money."

He said, "You have already been paid."

I replied, "I have not." He hastily pulled a timetable out of his pocket and showed me where it read: "from Chicago to Los Angeles and/or San Francisco—$46.00." I conceded meekly, "You win, Dick."

We took an apartment at a recommended place in San Francisco. It was run by a German-born woman who seemed right from the beginning to be very stern. After showing us our one room with kitchenette, bath and Murphy bed she said, "Don't send your laundry to the Chinese, they are unsanitary." She continued, "Use my laundry." It was plain to see that she was getting a rake-off from the American laundry. She put a cot in the room for Adrienne at an extra cost. Ena was now pregnant again and was feeling more uncomfortable than she did during her last pregnancy.

During the day Ena, Adrienne and I would go for long drives. We visited twin peaks near the center of San Francisco, where there was a beautiful view of the city. You could see the Golden Gate Bridge to the north and the long bridge to Oakland to the east. We visited Joe DiMaggio's place and Fisherman's Wharf. We crossed the Golden Gate Bridge and visited the huge redwood forest to the north. We took rides on the cable cars and often stood and watched them turn around on their turntables. The roads were so hilly and steep that often, instead of a sidewalk, there would be steps. The brakes on my car wore out prematurely.

The job was going well—no pressure at all and everyone was relaxed. We had a high-powered brass section, a good sax section, and good rhythm section with a bass player who was far superior to any of Goodman's bass players except for Artie Bernstein, who had come in at the tail end of his first band. Ena and Adrienne were waiting for me one day in the lobby of the posh St Francis Hotel while I finished a rehearsal. Himber was the first one to reach the lobby and he walked over to Ena, took his thumb and smeared her lipstick over her chin. She immediately hauled off and hit him a hard slap on the face, which resounded throughout the lobby. That was his weird idea of fun. He turned around with his diabolical, crooked, white-toothed smile.

One afternoon I had been out on an errand and I walked into the lobby of the apartment house and saw the elevator stuck between the lobby and the second floor. It was an elevator with a wrought-iron grille. Ena and Adrienne were sitting on the floor of the elevator, about a foot and a half of their bodies visible. They ducked their heads down and saw me. I said, "We'll get you out of there soon, honey." The landlady came rushing out and I told her to call the elevator company. She was flustered, but called the company right away. Ena and Adrienne sat calmly and patiently on the floor. The landlady was upset; she knew that Ena was pregnant. When, an hour and a half later, they were freed, the landlady couldn't do enough for us. I know now that I could have sued for plenty of money due to Ena's condition, but at that time I was just happy to see them safe and sound.

We finished at the St Francis Hotel on 31 March 1941, packed and left for Hollywood. On the way we went off the route to visit the huge redwood trees southeast of San Francisco. The altitude was high and, though it was the beginning of April, there was snow still on the ground. We were in a complete wilderness surrounded by those huge trees. We went down into a small gully where the snow was about four inches deep. We took pictures of Adrienne standing in front of a giant redwood; she looked like a little peanut.

We got back into the car, turned around and started up the slight rise, but got stuck in the snow. As we were miles from any habitation I said to Ena, "What do we do now?" She was a very resourceful girl and thought for a moment and finally exclaimed, "Why not wrap your pyjamas around the tires to act as sort of a chain."

"Good idea," I agreed. She opened a suitcase and pulled out my flannel pyjamas, which we then wrapped through an opening in the rear wheels after removing the hub caps. After a few tries we were on our way to a level spot. I removed the chewed-up pyjamas from the wheels and ran back for the hub caps. We were soon on our way south again. About fifteen miles on we came to the forest ranger's large booth and he stopped us. He inquired where we had come from and we explained to him that we had entered through the northwest side and had been stuck some fifteen miles away near the redwoods. He said, "Are you lucky. We don't patrol there except about once a month." He continued, "If you hadn't starved to death, the wild animals would have gotten you." We shrugged him off and calmly started driving south again with absolutely no fear in our hearts.

We arrived in Hollywood and checked into an apartment next to the Columbia Picture Studios. After only one rehearsal we opened on April 2nd at the Palladium Ballroom. Benny would have envied this great band. We had black arrangers including Freddy Norman. We had "Big" George Wendt on first trumpet, who could almost equal Ziggy's swing and volume. Bruce Squires and Red Ballard were on trombones. Red, who had been shy with Benny, lost all of his inhibitions and played fantastically well. Himber would let them try to cut each other and play chorus after chorus. These men inspired me to play better, and Joe Viola, our jazz clarinet player, played exceptionally well. It was really a great band, but short-lived.

One night at the Palladium a girl came in, beautifully dressed and very attractive, but obviously of tainted character and slightly drunk. I thought that I recognized her from our first year at the Palomar with Goodman. She came over to the bandstand, and when we finished a set I got off the stand and spoke to her. I queried, "Don't I know you from the Palomar, when you came in with Mr Kelly?"

She said, "Oh yes, any friend of Kelly's is a friend of mine." She became very chummy, her large bust heaving as she spoke. I walked towards the men's room and she started to follow me and waited for me at the men's room door. All evening I couldn't ditch her. I was worried because Ena often drove the block and a half to meet me in the side lobby of the Palladium. She would arrive at precisely 1 a.m., when we finished, leaving Adrienne a few minutes in the apartment sleeping, and we usually drove right home.

That night Ena waited for me as she often did. I told this girl, whose name I did not know and who was half drunk by now, that my wife was waiting for me. We had finished the last set, packed our instruments, and put them in the bandroom. (We did not have a band-boy. We did no one-nighters.) The boys saw Ena waiting in the side lobby. Artie Friedman and Dick Judge each grabbed one of the girl's arms and led her out towards the main lobby, and all the while she screamed, "I want Artie! I want Artie!" They finally dragged her out the front door and I joined Ena, never telling her about the experience that I had had. We drove to the apartment and went to bed.

The next day Ena and Adrienne were walking past Columbia Picture Studios next-door to our apartment and two directors stopped them and admired Adrienne; she was a beautiful child now, three and a half years old, and resembled Shirley Temple as a child star. They wanted to arrange a screen test for Adrienne. They gave Ena a number to call and Ena told them that she would talk it over with me. That evening we discussed the situation. I knew that very few people make it in Hollywood and, besides, Ena was pregnant, so we decided against it. The next day I called the number and refused the offer.

That night Ena came to the side lobby entrance to meet me at finishing time. I had had my instruments put away and walked out to the lobby to meet her. A young man was writhing on the floor clutching his stomach. He sobbed loudly, "Help me, please help me, I'm starving. I haven't eaten in a week." He continued to writhe and clutch his stomach.

I said to him, "I'll go into the kitchen and get you a ham sandwich."

He said, "I hate ham."

I yelled at him, "You phony, get the hell out of here." He got up and ran. Anyone knows that a starving person will eat almost anything.

We did a couple more Studebaker transcriptions during the day and finished at the Palladium on May 15th. Himber announced that we were to have a week's layoff. I called him aside and said, "No dice Dick. I was hired at X number of dollars for the trip and, if I don't get paid for the layoff, I am leaving for New York."

He replied, "You're not going to be paid."

I said, "You'll see!"

Ena and I talked it over that night and Ena, as usual, came up with an ingenious idea. She said excitedly, "Let's empty out all our luggage (a little was still remaining in the cases), pile the cases on the back seat of the car and go to his motel." We did so and Himber was home. I knocked on his door and he appeared in his robe. I extended my hand and said, "So long Dick, we are leaving for New York."

He replied, "Come on now, you're not going anyplace."

I said, "If you don't believe me, look out of the window." The profile of my car was visible outside the window, bags piled to the roof. He hemmed and hawed, went to the telephone and made an imaginary phone call to another tenor man—there was nobody on the other end of the line. He said to his imaginary tenor man, "Can you start next week at the LA Theatre? You can? Good." Ena and I started towards the door. Adrienne was waiting in the car. I opened the door and Ena stepped out. I said, "So long Dick," extending my hand to him.

He ordered, "Come back here." He walked back into his office room and sat down at his desk. He reluctantly wrote out a salary check, but he would not give me the satisfaction of handing it to me—he handed it to Ena. I grunted and said, "See you next week at the theater." Ena and I giggled all the way back to the apartment. We had outfoxed him. We took our bags out of the car and packed for our vacation.

We headed for the Mojave desert the next morning, and the weather was beautiful. The desert, where many Western pictures are filmed, was an ideal setting for my 16 mm color movies; the rocks were a reddish-brown color. We stopped at Red Rock

Canyon. The only person in sight was a man with a pony. I gave him a couple of dollars and I took some film with Adrienne riding the pony with the beautiful red rock formations in the vast background.

The next morning we arose very early and headed for Death Valley, a considerable distance away, since we were to enter at the northwest end. The scenery was beautiful and the altitude was high, about 5000 feet. We entered the valley; I was driving and Ena was filming as we started our descent. Ena filmed the markers along the road: 5000 feet, 4000 feet, 3000 feet, 2000 feet, 1000 feet and finally sea level. We had our windows fully open and could feel the hot dry air on our faces. We stopped at a little stand that was preparing to close for the season. I ordered three bottles of root beer, which was very refreshing in this broiling heat. I glanced at a thermometer: it was 117 degrees fahrenheit in the shade. We did not perspire because there was little or no humidity, just a blast of hot air. To our left were vast sand dunes. Not a single car passed and, because the season was over the previous day, everything would be closed for the next 150 miles. We decided to go on. We proceeded eastwards across the northern end of the valley. We took movies of abandoned covered wagons—borax wagons—and then proceeded southwards on the eastern side of the valley, passing Furnace Creek Camp and Furnace Creek Inn, both closed.

We had traveled halfway down the valley and the heat was almost unbearable. Adrienne was complaining about her thirst. I jokingly said to her, "Lick your lips honey." She looked at me quizzically and did as she was told. She was a good trooper. We reached Badwater, about halfway down the length of the valley. We were now at the lowest point in the Western Hemisphere, 279.6 feet below sea level. The car started to boil over and simultaneously we got a flat tire. "What do we do now?" I thought. We let the car cool off a couple of hours, Adrienne complaining more and more about her thirst. Here I was, no water in the radiator, a flat tire, a pregnant wife and a small child.

While we were waiting I filmed a natural stone bridge spanning a thirty- or forty-foot natural stone bed. I took a temperature reading under the bridge: 125 degrees in the shade. Across the valley, some ten miles away, we could see the towering snow-capped mountains, some of them jutting over 10,000 feet into the sky, with Telescope Peak, the leader, 11,200 feet in altitude. Here we were at Badwater, a small pond with brackish, poisonous, alkaline water. Numerous forty-niners had died after drinking this water during the gold rush.

I went back to the car after filming the sea-level marker far above us. I also photographed the awesome mountains on the other side of the valley. I said to Ena, "Now, let's get to work." Meanwhile not a single car had passed; there was not a moving thing in sight, except an occasional salamander. I opened the car trunk and pulled out the spare tire, jacked up the car and mounted the tire. I released the jack and the car sank. There were only about ten pounds of air in the spare. I had no tire pump. I looked at the sleezy, brackish water, which looked stagnant even with all its foliage; it looked ominous. Ena exclaimed excitedly, "Let's try some in the radiator."

I replied, "OK, what can we lose? We can't stay here or we'll die." I began to perspire profusely. Adrienne had tears in her eyes. Fortunately Adrienne had her little beach pail in the trunk of the car and I scooped up this terrible water. As I filled the radiator Ena turned on the engine.

I looked at the road map and saw a place called Bradbury's Well some distance south. We thought that we would see some habitation. We proceeded slowly, our left rear tire feeling mushy with so little air in it, and finally arrived at Bradbury's Well. We drove off to the left of the road and parked. Not a soul in sight. After walking up a slight rise we found the well. There was a heavy rope two inches in diameter extending into the well. I pulled on the rope and up came a large bucket. My God! It had a hole in it two and a half inches in diameter. Ena said quickly, "Get the beach pail." By now Adrienne was sobbing from intense thirst. It was about 125 degrees here also in the shade of the car.

I untied the cumbersome rope and fastened it to the little pail, lowered it into the well and pulled it up. Ena tasted the water. It seemed OK. She waited a few minutes with no ill effects and gave some to Adrienne and me. We drank just enough to satisfy our immediate thirst. Meanwhile I was taking color movies of all the action. I drained the radiator of the sludgy water and made many trips back and forth while filling the radiator. Adrienne felt better now, although she was still thirsty.

We headed southwards again, slowly because of the tire. It was beginning to get dark, as the sun had disappeared over the high peaks in the west. We plodded on and finally came to a hill, and, after a long climb, we were out of the valley. At the southeast end we saw lights. It was now almost dark. We found a small hotel, parked and locked the car. The hotel coffee-shop was still open. First we asked for water. Little Adrienne drank three full glasses, Ena and I not far behind. We ate a nice meal and enjoyed it since we had had no lunch. We all felt better now and checked into this small hotel. Ena and Adrienne went to the room and I got the bag out of the car, leaving the less than half inflated tire alone. We quickly prepared for bed. It was amazingly cooler now and we slept well.

The next morning we arose rather early and each of us took a well needed bath. After breakfast I went to a service station, pumped up my tire and left the other tire to be repaired. While they were doing this I walked up to a general store and stocked up with a tire pump, flares, trouble light and a canteen, which we fortunately never had to use. I picked up my repaired tire, filled the tank with gas (it was only $1.00 for eight gallons of high test), checked the oil and went back to the hotel, where Ena had packed our bag with our meager overnight clothes, and we checked out.

On the way back to Hollywood that afternoon we stopped at a beautiful trout stream. The air temperature was about 72 degrees, just perfect, and we chose a beautiful spot to film. I took out my tripod and set up the camera with Ena and Adrienne sitting near this beautiful clear stream with snow-capped mountains in the background and eucalyptus trees on the left. Ena and Adrienne threw pebbles into the stream. I set the camera and even joined them in a scene. I was sorry that I didn't have my fishing rod with me because the stream was teeming with fish, which were leaping out of the water. We spent the afternoon there and arrived at our apartment in Hollywood at nightfall. What a lovely day it had been!

The next morning I called Joe Viola and Eddie Stone. They asked, "Where in hell have you been?"

I replied casually, "Death Valley."

Came Mother's Day 1941. Ena, Adrienne and I were eating at a drive-in stand when we saw a man selling little yellow ducklings, each wearing a little hat and harness. He sold them in a quart ice-cream container with seed. I bought one for Ena for Mother's Day. We took it home and Ena removed the hat and harness to make it, a male, more comfortable. The duckling would follow us all over the apartment. I would run from room to room, turning the corner suddenly. The little duck would run after me and turn corners on one leg like a Keystone Comedy character. Ena made a terrible mistake one day, however. She put the duck in the bath tub of lukewarm water. It swam beautifully, but developed pneumonia the next day. Ena kept it in a warm place and swabbed its nostrils constantly and in several days nursed it back to health. It had its own carton with seed, lettuce (which it loved) and water. Ena never should have put it in water at such an early age because its undeveloped feathers did not have oil on them yet.

We opened at the Los Angeles Theatre for two weeks. The band was cooking and Himber featured his magic tricks and impersonations. The boys and I would mess up his tricks between shows. He would imitate Charles Boyer on the telephone—he even looked like Boyer. He had a phone on stage with a long clothes-line dyed black, leading backstage. He would pick up the phone and say, in a French accent, "Thees ees Sharles Boyay," and would go into a phone conversation. I sneaked in between shows and cut the cord about eight inches from the phone. The next show he went into his Boyer act. He said, "Hello, thees ees Sharles Boyay." About eight inches of cord hung from the phone. After the curtain came down he screamed, "Who did that?" I never owned up.

We finished at the theater and did a two-reel short of twenty minutes duration. It featured the band on a stage with mirrors on three sides. The mirrors made the band look three times its size. I was featured in every number and the cameras constantly photographed me, while Himber stood impatiently behind the cameras with his makeup on, waiting to be photographed. The film was scheduled to be completed in two days. Himber paced back and forth while they photographed me. Came the afternoon of the second day, Himber was still waiting to go on, and they continued close-ups of me. During a pause I said to him, "Stick around Dick, and maybe I'll give you a small part in my picture." At the very end they got a brief shot of the back of Himber's head while he was conducting the band.

We were finished in Hollywood. Ena packed our things; Himber gave me $75 car money, so my records show. The four boys and Himber took the train to New York and Ena, Adrienne and I drove along with our duckling, who was in the cardboard box on the floor in the back. We took the southern route through Arizona, turning 110 miles north to visit the Grand Canyon. We filmed the canyon and trailways. The visibility was excellent, although the sky was yellow; the colors were simply beautiful. We went up and down the rim of the canyon and stopped at a little mud hut. A little Indian boy came out and I asked him to pose for me. He was a good little businessman and wouldn't pose unless I gave him a quarter. I obliged.

We spent a few hours at the canyon photographing, then had a bite to eat and went back 110 miles to the main road and headed east. That night we left our duck in the car in its carton with the window partially open and checked into a motel in eastern Arizona. In the morning we awakened early. We had our window open and could hear our duck chirping happily. It was chirping "Cheetie pee, cheetie pee," and that is what we named it, "Cheetie Pee." We continued east and in Flagstaff, Arizona, which is about 7000 feet in altitude, we ran into a brief snow squall. We descended and continued on. Each morning when we awakened we would hear our duckling chirping happily. Even with the stop at the Grand Canyon we made it to New York in six days, Ena and I alternating the driving.

That was the end of my time with Himber so I thought, but it was not to be, as I later found out. I did not look for work immediately, but just waited for the phone to ring. I did club dates for the Lanin office, the Ben Cutler office and the Morse office, and a couple of record dates. I played the Paramount for three days and did a date for Stuart Allen, the singer. I was not doing a land-office business, but getting by without looking for work. I really wanted to acquaint myself with my new home that I

Benny Goodman's softball team, 1938: (back row, left to right) Bud Freeman, Chris Griffin, Harry Goodman, Arthur, Harry James, Ziggy Elman, Vernon Brown, Noni Bernardi; (front row, left to right) Benny Heller, Pee Wee Monte, Dave Tough, Red Ballard

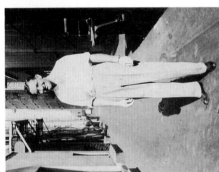

Far Left: Arthur, c1938. Left: Benny Goodman in Los Angeles, 1935. Below: Watching the Goodman softball team at Richmond, Virginia: (left to right) Harry Goodman, Hymie Shertzer, Benny, Arthur, Noni Bernardi

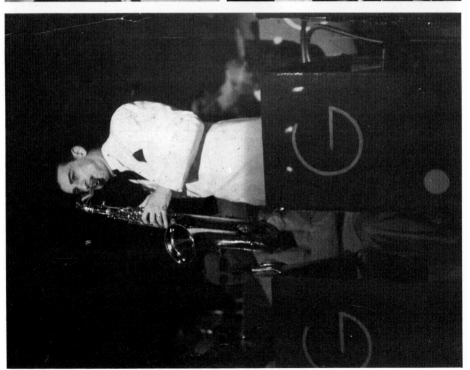

Ray McKinley

Will Bradley

Above: Arthur, 1941. Left: Harry Clark, Adrian Rollini and Frank Victor.

Top Left: Adrienne. Top Right: Ena. Left: Arthur, 1953, during his time in the ABC Staff Orchestra

Columbia Recording Studio, 22 October 1958, at the launching of the album *Treasure Chest of Performance Recordings*, from 1937–8. Above: Hymie Shertzer, Arthur, Vernon Brown, George Koenig, Goodman. Below: Shertzer, Brown, Arthur, Fletcher Henderson

To Art
with many fond
memories of our
collaboration during
the 30s — with
warm regards.
Benny

Benny Goodman, *c*1984

hardly had time to enjoy. In my spare time I did some carpentry work, which was my hobby.

On 19 July 1941 I did a job for Howard Lanin in Westchester County. We finished at 1 a.m., and by the time I packed and took the long trip to my home in Queens, it was about 2:30. I went right to bed. Ena awakened me at 5:30 a.m., saying that she had been in labor for two hours and was timing the pains. She had called Dr Watson, her obstetrician, and arranged to have him meet us an hour later. I said to her in a frenzy, "Why didn't you call me before this?"

She answered calmly, "I wanted you to get some sleep." Ena was ready and packed. I threw on my clothes and we rushed to the hospital in Jackson Heights. I know that I shouldn't have done this, but I went through every red light on the way. We met Dr Watson and he rushed Ena upstairs. I bought a Sunday newspaper and sat in the waiting room reading. I had glanced through about half my paper when Dr Watson came down the stairs, extended his hand and said, "Congratulations, it's a boy!" I beamed. It was now only 7:45. I saw Ena briefly and had a glimpse of our son. I went home happy. It had been rather a close call. Upon arrival at home I immediately undressed and went to bed and slept a little more. I visited Ena that afternoon and saw the baby again. I had a job that night with Willie Lanin, Howard's brother. After five days Ena was home.

SEVEN

The end of my thirty years

Meanwhile I received a call from Will Bradley's manager, Doc Richardson. He asked me if I wanted to join the band. After coming to terms I accepted. Will Bradley had been a busy freelance radio trombone player. He was also good looking, and the William Morris office had groomed him to front the band some time before. Ray McKinley, a fine drummer and novelty singer, was the co-leader. The band had more or less introduced boogie-woogie in big-band form. While at the Astor Hotel in New York they had fired the sax section, all but Mahlon Clark, a fine seventeen-year-old clarinet player, who years later married one of the Lennon sisters while they were with Lawrence Welk.

I replaced Peanuts Hucko on jazz tenor; in those days Peanuts would not play clarinet, even for backgrounds. He later went overseas with Glenn Miller in the armed forces and returned a good clarinet player. Goodman was his idol. Les Robinson, formerly with Artie Shaw, was on first alto, Clark on third alto and clarinet. I was on first tenor, Pete Mondello (Toots Mondello's cousin) on second tenor and Larry Molinelli on baritone. The brass consisted of Ralph Muzzillo, Steve Lipkins and Lee Castaldo (Castle) on trumpets and Bill Corti and Jimmy Emert on trombones. The rhythm section was Ray McKinley, drums, Billy Maxted, piano, Felix Giobbe, bass, and Steve Jordan, guitar.

The charts were now different, some written by black arrangers, and we suddenly developed into one of the top swing bands, playing boogie-woogie only upon request to my recollection. We finished at the Hotel Astor after four weeks. We worked a theater in Washington, DC, and then hit the road for a week of one-nighters. George Koenig had replaced Les Robinson, who didn't want to go on the road. George had played third alto for some time while I was with Goodman. On October 2nd we opened at the Sherman Hotel in Chicago for four weeks, then did two weeks of one-nighters and a split week in Akron and Youngstown, Ohio.

When we opened at a theater in Milwaukee for a week Ena came out with Adrienne, leaving our son with Mom at our house. I had seen Ena in Chicago and Youngstown before this, but hadn't seen Adrienne in quite awhile; she had grown and I was so pleased to see her. Just two days before I had to leave Milwaukee Ena and Adrienne contracted the flu, so I had to go to Fort Wayne, Indiana, and leave them behind. Pete Candoli had now joined the band on jazz trumpet, and Tommy di Carlo was also a member of the trumpet section.

A couple days after we opened at the theater in Fort Wayne, Ena and Adrienne arrived at the hotel after I had finished the early evening show. They looked pale and drawn and I sent down for some food. They ate very little. They soon went to bed and I went to the theater to play the last show. The following day we arose at 10 a.m., and turned on the radio. It was 7 December 1941, and we heard the news about Pearl Harbor. We were shocked, as many millions of people were. The radio kept blaring the fragmentary reports and soon it was time to go to the theater. I went down to the lobby and there were many people listening to the radio. It was the talk of Fort Wayne and every other town and city in the USA.

We played only one week in Fort Wayne. Ena and Adrienne went home, and we headed for a week of one-nighters throughout New England. While traveling by bus at night, when everyone was asleep, Bradley thought that it was great sport to awaken everyone by rolling empty Coca-cola bottles down the aisle. A great talent, however.

In New York we did a "soundie." This was a film which was shown in a machine similar to a TV set and was popular in bars. You would drop a dime in the machine, press a button, and watch a short show of perhaps six minutes duration, if my recollection is correct. Bradley and McKinley reputedly had recouped their losses and were ready to disband. This was the end of a fine and talented band.

Felix Giobbe suggested that I write to Chauncey Gray at the El

Morocco in New York. I did so later on, but in the meantime Himber called me and I did some dates for him in the New York area. He also booked a couple of weeks at Valley Dale across the river in New Jersey, near Frank Daley's Meadowbrook. The band went over well and Himber was back to his old habits.

One night he suggested that I take Ena to Valley Dale for a champagne party. We accepted. It was about an hour's drive and Ena looked elegant. Himber reserved a table for us near the bandstand and Ena sat down and listened to the band for the first set. I then joined her. A waiter brought out two champagne glasses and a split of champagne. We laughed in contempt at his stupidity. He was a non-drinker and non-smoker. Ena sipped her champagne and nursed it all evening. I had a couple swallows and went back on the bandstand. I did not speak to Himber the rest of the evening, and I sat directly behind him. Later in the evening he must have sensed that something was wrong, because he called our house the next day and invited Ena and Adrienne to go down to his office at the Pierre Hotel, saying that he had a surprise for them. They met him at the office at the designated time and he took them to Macy's department store, where he bought Adrienne (whom he adored) a complete outfit: hat, coat, dress, shoes and socks. That is the way he was.

Chauncey Gray called me. He said his tenor man was leaving and asked if I would start at the El Morocco. The money was poor, but he said the tips were good, so I agreed to join him. I must add that Chauncey Gray was the composer of *Bye Bye Blues*, the closing theme of the Bert Lown Band with which he had played years before. The hours were from 8 p.m. to 4 a.m., six nights a week. (I would arrive home at precisely 5:10 a.m. every morning after taking the subway and picking up my car at the 169th Street station in Jamaica.) We were to alternate with a Latin band twenty minutes on, twenty off, thirty on and thirty off, forty on and forty off, etc. The bands would interchange with a common theme and the boys would replace those in the other band one by one, so that there was continuous music for eight hours, one tempo. Businessman's bounce! On the ballads we would keep the same tempo but play in 2/2.

The band consisted of Tony Lippi, trumpet and mellophone, Jules Rubin, Charles Ponti and myself on saxes, plus rhythm section with Chauncey on piano and the guitar player doing the vocals. This job was tedious, but the tips were good at first. Tommy Manville would come in practically every night and he was good for at least $20. Other society people were the same. We were not allowed to sit with the clientele and had a locker room in the basement with the garbage cans. In sheer desperation, to break the monotony, I started to write out charts at my own expense and in my own time. Soon Chauncey paid me a small fee for writing. We also recorded a couple of my charts.

One night while I was going to work there was a severe storm. I parked my car at the subway station and ran for cover in the teeming rain. Upon returning to my car at 5 a.m. I found that I had locked the door and left the bright lights on with the engine running. The battery was dead, the gasoline was all gone and there was no car key—I had left it in the car. I had to walk one and a half miles home in the rain because there were no cabs at that hour. When I got home, Ena, who usually lay on the living room couch sleeping while waiting for me, had become alarmed when I was so late. She had been pacing back and forth in the living room. I told her what had happened and she was relieved. The next day I had to take a cab back to the car, get a locksmith to open it, charge the battery and fill my tank with gas.

I was terribly disillusioned. I had been at the El Morocco for about five months by now and the grind was getting to me. The tips were getting smaller and smaller. One night my cousin Mimo, Maxmillian Cianfarra, the Rome correspondent for the *New York Times*, came in with his wife and another couple just as we were finishing a set. He came over to the bandstand and invited me over for a drink, saying that he had been transferred to Mexico City. He just wanted to say goodbye. I said to myself, "What the hell, rules or no rules, I am going to the table." We had one fast drink. They were there only twenty minutes and he was presented with a check for $20. He asked the waiter, "What is this?"

The waiter replied, "Mostly cover charge." Mimo asked me to see if I could knock off the cover charge, but I was helpless in this place.

They soon left and I was never to see my cousin again, for he was later transferred back to Rome. During the 1950s he was on his way to New York on the *Andrea Doria* for a grand reunion when the Swedish ship *Stockholm* struck his cabin and he perished. His young daughter was scooped onto the bow of the other ship, which was smaller in size, and was miraculously unharmed; his wife survived also.

We suspected that Chauncey was holding out on the tips. I don't know for sure, but instead of saying that he received a $20 bill, he would pull out a $5 bill from the other little inner jacket pocket. One night a customer requested a number and Julie Rubin was the only one who knew it. Chauncey got a good tip and withheld it. I was completely disillusioned.

I began to double tea sessions at the Stork Club with Ted Steele and subs at the Roxy Theatre with Paul Ash, plus recordings. I finally gave my notice, but that was not the last time I saw Chauncey Gray. I had been at the El Morocco from 4 March until 27 October 1942. I then joined Paul Ash at the Roxy Theatre; he had been there for years. I would substitute for a different sax player every day because, due to union rules, men were not allowed to work the seven days.

Himber called me and asked if I would go to Florida for ten days. The money was good, so I accepted. The date was in Tampa, Florida, from 13 to 22 November and, although Himber was a character, I enjoyed the relaxation. Some of the boys took their wives; I didn't. I took my movie camera with me, however. Hy Small and Walter Mercurio were on this date. When I came home I worked full time at the Roxy Theatre until Paul Ash's contract was up, then as a freelance almost every day until 1943.

I was called for an Ethel Merman show which was to open on Broadway on January 2nd. The show was a great war comedy called *Something for the Boys*. The work was easy, but became boring because of its sameness; I had memorized the thick book in three weeks. Between scenes and Merman's vocals we would play checkers and cards in the pit. The evening hours were from 8:40 p.m. to 11 p.m., with two matinees, Wednesday and Saturday. I had several solos to play but, even though the show was a hit, I became bored after a couple months. When you accept a show, however, you are required to stay for the duration.

One day before a matinee I saw Paul Ricci, a fine tenor and clarinet man, and he asked me if I would like to replace him at

CBS, where he was with Raymond Scott. I was desperate by now with the sameness of this show (it eventually ran for one and a half years). I asked the conductor, a gray-haired gent (I do not remember his name), if I could leave. He said, "No." I bugged him over and over again but he was adamant. Finally he conceded a little and said, "If you can find me a suitable replacement, I'll let you leave." I sent four different men in at my expense and he was dissatisfied. He finally said, "If you can get me the right man and write out some solos for him, I'll let you go." I wrote out some solos. Previously, I would play above the register of the tenor sax and had to keep within range. I called Herman Wolfson, a tenor man who had played with Himber long before me, and he was accepted. I was happy.

I called Paul Ricci and asked him when I would start at CBS with Raymond Scott. He was elated, but I didn't know why. He said, "Tomorrow morning." I asked him about the money and he mentioned a high figure for those days. This band was being paid well because it was on a week-to-week basis.

I started on 1 April 1943. The job consisted of a fifteen-minute morning show with a one-hour rehearsal. That was it! Perry Como was vocalist, Tony Mattola on guitar, Cozy Cole on drums, Hank D'Amico on third alto and clarinet, Artie Baker (also a good clarinet player) on first alto, Eddie Brown on fourth tenor, oboe and English horn, Red Soloman on trumpet, Johnny Guarnieri on piano and Gene Traxler on bass. Small band.

The first morning when I arrived in the studio at CBS Scott opened the windows and asked us to take breathing exercises. Afterwards we sat down and he gave directions from the control booth. Red Soloman was his official demonstrator. Scott would ask Red to show Perry Como how to sing a certain phrase. He would ask Red over the intercom to show Cozy Cole a certain beat. He said to Eddie Brown, "Eddie, your horn is too out of chune for practical purposes. I suggest that you have it adjusted." He went down the line. No wonder Paul Ricci quit. I could see now that Scott was seemingly an eccentric person, but a fine musician.

Finally, one morning, I had the tenor lead on a four-sax passage. We went over it a few times and he stopped the band. Scott (in the control room) suddenly said to me, "Art, step to the mike and play *Body and Soul.*" I played it. He said, "OK."

I asked, "What's wrong, Harry?" That was his real name, Harry Warnow.

He replied, "Nothing." *Body and Soul* wasn't even on the show. We went on the show cold having rehearsed only four bars.

The next day we fiddled around and went on the air cold again. In the middle of the show he held a piano copy of *I could have cried all night* in front of my face, his hands trembling. I had never played this song before and the changes were unusual for those days. I got through it OK. We seldom rehearsed. Scott would dwell on a few bars and we would go on the show cold.

By the next week I had had it. On the Wednesday Frank Vagnoni of NBC called me and asked me if I could get away. I replied, "Definitely. We are on a week-to-week basis with no notice required."

Vagnoni said, "Fine, you start Monday at NBC on staff, but I am going to give you an extra show before that, this Saturday."

I said, "Fine."

On Thursday of the second week at CBS I told Lou Shoobie, the contractor, that I was leaving the next day. He said to me, "You at least could have given me a little notice."

I said, "Lou, remember, we are on a week-to-week basis." But he was teed off and called me only once after that when he was stuck. I believe Ben Webster followed me. I pitied him.

I started the next day, 10 May 1943, with NBC, doing a special show, and on Monday started the staff job with Frank Vagnoni where I was to remain for fourteen and a half years. I started studying flute in earnest with Henry Zlotnick on 48th Street, opposite Manny's Music Store and the Musical Instrument Exchange. The whole block was dotted with music stores, where I bought many hundreds and thousands of saxophone reeds. I would often practice flute and piccolo three or four hours a day, sometimes more.

We were allowed to work only five days a week according to union rules, but Frank Vagnoni would often change my days off so that I could do a recording session. He was indeed a remarkable, understanding and considerate man.

Bernie Mann called me to play weekends at his Tip Top Club in

Flushing. I was to be the leader and could, as such, work seven days a week. I told Bernie that he would have to hire the men and have the musical arrangements made, which he did. He hired the men and had Freddy Weismantel make many charts for my eight-piece group. The band consisted of Skippy Lipsey on trumpet, plus trombone, and myself on tenor sax. We had a four-piece rhythm section including Ted Kotsoftis on bass and Steve Jordan (who had worked with me before in the Will Bradley band) on guitar. We had a girl vocalist named Sally Ayres, who was good.

The Tip Top Club teemed with beautiful girls, but most of the young men were now in the army. I never dated any of these girls and one night Bernie remarked to me, "Art, I admire you, you never s—t where you sleep." This made me feel good, as I loved Ena dearly. Saturday nights were difficult at the Tip Top because we finished at 3 a.m., and I had to be up at seven Sunday mornings to do a kiddie's radio show at NBC which went on the air at nine. After the show, however, I would often go home and take a nap for an hour or so. Ena was unhappy as I was seldom home, except to sleep.

I had long since been placed in category 1A by the draft board. Frank Vagnoni had his chief secretary, Margie Lubiere (of French Canadian extraction), write a letter to my draft board saying that I was essential to the network, doing a radio broadcast called "This Nation at War" beamed to the armed forces. The draft board promptly put me in 3A.

I kept studying flute in my spare time and Frank Vagnoni put me on "Saludos Amigos," a program which featured Spanish music exclusively. I played nothing but flute on this show. The music was difficult and I would often go to the network library and take the flute book to a small empty studio for study. Henry Zlotnick, my flute teacher, also a fine piccolo player, often remarked that I was doing well. He would say to me, "I have to work a little harder to keep up with my students." I ordered a Powell flute, open-hole with a low B foot joint, which had to be put on special order. I had been playing a Haynes closed-hole flute.

One Friday night I invited Ena to the Tip Top Club. We sat down at a table near the bar, when suddenly a young girl came over to the table and introduced herself as Ginger Peppi. She said, "Hello Art, I am your new vocalist, I'm sure that we will get along beautifully." (Sally Ayres had left.) Ena was a little taken back by this and I could see that she was perturbed. Ginger was attractive, young and had a sparkling personality. Ginger and I worked together for almost two years, during which time she would come down to the studios to catch the rehearsals. She also called at our house occasionally on one pretense or another. I was fond of her, but never dated her. One day after a rehearsal I completely ignored her and she took a taxi to Pennsylvania Station with one of the trombone players. He became a little amorous in the cab and she bent his fingers back. I found out about this the following day.

Meanwhile NBC formed two networks, the Red, NBC, and the Blue, ABC. I was to remain with the latter for many years. We were extremely busy at the network, and I practiced and practiced, often between rehearsals and the show. Many of the other boys would go to Hurley's Bar at the corner of 49th Street and Seventh Avenue for a few drinks. I would find a small studio and work.

One afternoon I was studying in a small studio in NBC next to studio 8H, where the great Toscanini had been rehearsing the NBC orchestra and was now resting. There was a knock on the door of the studio and I opened it. It was Toscanini's representative. I asked him to enter. He said, "Mr Toscanini is resting and must have complete quiet."

I quickly responded, "Tell Mr Toscanini that I must practice." He left and I continued with a more subdued sound. They never bothered me again.

I was doing "The Hildegarde Show," "The Jack Benny Show" (when he was in town), and "The Kate Smith Show" occasionally, as well as recordings and transcriptions when I could squeeze them in. Paul Whiteman came to the Blue Network as musical director with an eight-year contract. He asked for me.

On 22 June 1944 we went to Philadelphia to do the "Philco Hall of Fame" show. We were all, I believe, twenty-eight of us, introduced to Leopold Stokowski, the great conductor of the Philadelphia Orchestra. As we were introduced he said, "How do you do, please do not squeeze the hand." We finished our

"Philco" broadcast and went back to our train. I saw Frank Vagnoni and he was looped; I observed him staggering into the ladies' room. It was the one and only time that I had ever seen him in this condition. I was happy for Frank, because he always worked so hard in preparing his weekly schedule, which, with sixty-five men on staff, was huge.

I was working day and night. The Tip Top Club had been sold and we finished on 17th June. Bernie Mann had bought the Riviera in Manhasset, and trumpet player Mel Conner was the leader of the five-piece group. On the last night at the Tip Top Ginger asked me to take her home to Valley Stream, where she lived with her mother. I said, "Honey, I can't take you home, I have to be up at 7 a.m. for 'The Kiddie Show.'" She begged. I compromised and said, "I'll take you to the Jamaica station, where you can take a bus to Valley Stream." Hithertofore she had always gotten a ride with one of the waiters. We reached the bus station and we sat in the car for half an hour before her bus arrived. It was plain to see that this girl was fond of me. I was fond of her, but hands off!

I did dates with Louis Armstrong, Russ Morgan and Joe Stopak. It seemed like I was doing some of the best work in New York! Time went on at ABC. Whiteman had me playing tenor sax, clarinet, bass clarinet, flute, piccolo and bass saxophone (the last-named I borrowed from Adrian). We took cabs from the studio and I managed to carry everything in one clip on the way to the Ritz Theatre. We had many guests on the "Philco Hall of Fame" show, including Ronald Coleman, Peggy Lee, Jo Stafford, Milton Berle, Alexis Smith, Jack Carter, and even Adrian with his trio. I sat in the control room and balanced the trio. Adrian was paid well and received a beautiful plaque from Philco.

Ena had had frequent asthma attacks, a tendency which she had inherited from her mother and grandmother, but between attacks was a great housekeeper. I would find the baby grand piano moved from place to place where she moved it by herself on her strong shoulders. She was now studying piano and voice; her idols at that time were Mildred Bailey (of Whiteman Fame) and Ella Fitzgerald.

My neighbour Sid Stoneburn, a good clarinet player, was also on the "Philco" show. He had to play the opening clarinet cadenza from Gershwin's *Rhapsody in Blue* while in a glass cage, a terribly scarey thing. We were very good friends. Sid lived about a mile or so from me and we would car pool to the Kew Gardens subway station, where we would take the subway to Radio City, getting off at the 49th Street station. One night he flubbed the cadenza and received his eight-week notice. Then Al Gallodoro, in my estimation the best technician of our day, was called in on staff to play alto sax, clarinet and bass clarinet. Sid was demoted. Al Gallodoro had been with the Whiteman band before and knew the routine beautifully. This man could read and transpose almost anything; he was a self-taught musician and would often practice six or eight hours a day. He could double tongue, triple tongue on alto with ease and was magnificent. We became fast friends.

One night, when Sid and I were returning to my car at Kew Gardens, we stopped at a bar across the street and were drinking a beer. Two young men were playing the jukebox and had selected Will Bradley's *Request for a Rhumba*, which we had recorded in 1941. They played it over and over. Finally I stepped off the bar stool and asked, "Boys, why are you playing that record over and over?"

One of them replied, "We like the tenor sax solo." I felt elated, but did not tell them that it was I who played it.

Meanwhile Ena was having more severe asthma attacks and I called Dr Bruno Waldman in to attend to her. Bruno and I became fast friends and he asked me to teach him to play clarinet. He asked me to pick up a used clarinet for him, so I went to Manny's on 48th Street and tried all of his used clarinets. I finally came up with a French make, a Robert. He gave the $90 which I had paid and said, "Don't tell my wife, she thinks I paid $40." As "The Kiddie Show" was now finished, Dr Waldman would come over to my home on Sunday mornings, and he would study. This man had a photographic memory and in three short months had mastered the clarinet fingerings from top to bottom. Then one Sunday he called me and said, "Mr Rollini, I have a flu epidemic on my hands and cannot study any longer." I said, "OK, Bruno, I understand."

I continued studying flute in every spare moment and soon my teacher couldn't keep up with me. Not that I was better, because

Henry was a fine flute player—a Barrère student—but, due to the fact that he was not too familiar with these advanced studies and had many students, he was unable to practice all of the intricate exercises. I stayed with Henry six or seven years.

As most people know there were many boo-boos during the early days of radio. Shortly after leaving Goodman, Martha Tilton was doing a guest spot on a radio show in New York. When she visited Ena and me in our new home in Jamaica Estates North Martha came up with a story about the program on which she was featured. On this show (there was no tape then) the announcer blurted, "Here comes private Smith with a purple heart on." This one broke up the audience. (This was war time.)

Subsequently I witnessed a few boo-boos myself, such as one on a program for newly retired people. The announcer asked the gentleman, "Now, what do you do in all your spare time?"

The gent replied, "Oh, I just fart around all day." On another show, dedicated to lonely war brides, the announcer asked a bride, "What would you like more than anything else in the world?"

She replied with little hesitation, "I would like to wake up one morning with my husband standing by the bed with a discharge in his hand." Naturally this broke up the audience. She piped up, "I don't mean that kind of a discharge!" Everyone howled, and the station was cut off the air. After a brief pause an announcer came back on the air and said, "There will now be a short organ recital!" Such were the days before tape.

I guess everyone knows the story about Uncle Don, who featured a kiddie show on WOR every evening at 6 p.m. He spoke to the kiddies with a saccharin voice for fifteen minutes. One night, upon completion of his show, he thought that he was off the air and inadvertently blurted, "I guess that that will hold the little bastards for a while." To my knowledge Uncle Don was never heard from again.

Whiteman was very congenial to me; the men were afraid of him, but I had no fear. At rehearsal on Saturday for the "Philco" show he would have his assistant conductor. First this was Teddy Dale, who would often have tears in his eyes when hearing the rendition of his fine arrangements by this great orchestra. Teddy was admired by every arranger in the country. He did not stay too long, however, as he found writing a ten-minute overture every week to be exhausting. He would conduct the rehearsal and Whiteman had the overture recorded to take home for study so that he would be fully prepared for the Sunday afternoon rehearsal. After Teddy Dale left Abe Osser took over. Abe had absolute pitch and could write much faster than Teddy Dale, but not so fluently. He would write the cue music for the "Script" shows on the train on the way to New York from Harrison, Westchester County, and the parts would be ready for us at rehearsal. In the beginning he was very awkward as a conductor. All the boys liked Abe and I worked with him for a long time. He had such a keen ear that he could detect a wrong passing note by one of the obscure violinists and call out the right one. He was calm, never got excited, and was always efficient.

Whiteman had many expressions that I remember to this day. At rehearsal on Sunday he would say to the strings, "Stop sawing off the roundsteak." Or he would say, "That sounds like a bag of worms." He would say to the brass section, who were saving their lips for the show, "Blow, don't suck!" On a dance number he would beat off, instead of "One and two," he would say "Uhvuva, uhvuva." He was indeed a comical man. At one rehearsal for "Philco," Whiteman gave a quick, unexpected downbeat. Nobody played. He bellowed, "What do you think I'm doing this for? (waving his baton wildly). Do you think I have the quaking palsy or something?" I believe we did the "Philco" show for three years, and Whiteman was always congenial to me.

By this time I was overworked, going from studio to studio. Dick Ridgely joined the orchestra, having left station WOR, and was now our auxiliary drummer, playing xylophone, timpani, vibes and chimes. George Wettling was in the first drum chair, playing fine drums when he was sober. After hours he would drink and become absolutely impossible; he had a mild tempered nature, but when he drank, he was mean. On another show we had to lock him out of the studio and he banged on the door while we were on the air.

Al Gallodoro was on first alto, I was on second tenor, Hank D'Amico was on third sax and jazz clarinet, Herman Yorks was on fourth tenor, doubling flute, clarinet and bassoon, and Irving Horowitz was on fifth baritone, doubling flute, bass clarinet and magnificent oboe and english horn. In the brass section we had "Spots" George Esposito on first trumpet, the Morreale brothers, Jim and Jack (also on trumpet), and Charlie Small and Vernon Brown on trombone (the latter from the Goodman band). We had Leo Kahn and Maxie Cahn on violins, Alfred Corrado on french horn, Gloria Agostino on harp and Molly Dolittle on cello. A couple of other names slip my mind at this time, but it was a great orchestra. Felix Giobbe was on bass and, of course, Mike Pingitore on guitar. We had almost finished the "Philco" run when Buddy Weed, a fine pianist, joined us. Buddy was not only a good jazz pianist but a fine concert pianist as well.

On 21 May 1945 I was called for the draft. I had suddenly been placed in category 1A. I went down for my army physical and we had an invasion of Japan to face. Germany had already surrendered on May 8th. Ena was perturbed, as I was accepted. That night I went home with mixed emotions. I knew that I was healthy and could probably get a job with an army band after basic training. We made preparations and everything was set. Three days later we were listening to the news on radio and they declared that no men thirty years or older with children born before Pearl Harbor would be drafted. Ena was relieved!

The "Stop the Music" show with Bert Parks started with Harry Salter and Ted Raph conducting. Bert Parks did a creditable job as host and was a wonderful guy. This show was a great hassle, as we were constantly changing instruments and the music in our book, plus we had the "Mystery Melody," which was pasted on the top of our books. The mystery melodies were hard to recognize and after a while clues were reported in the newspaper. There were very few big winners.

This show went on for about five years. It was an ordeal for me with my extra work. After a while with this routine I found that I couldn't fall asleep at night; many a night I would lie awake with no sleep whatsoever. One night after "Stop the Music" I arrived home with severe pains in my chest. Adrian and Dixie had been visiting that day. I did not drink, but Adrian made me three whiskey and milk concoctions. I became violently ill and went to bed, vomiting frequently. In the morning Ena called Frank Vagnoni and mistakenly told him that I had had a nervous breakdown. Actually it was a nervous collapse: I hadn't had any sleep for days.

Adrian was leaving for Florida that day to go to his fishing lodge in Tavernier, on Key Largo, where he had accommodations for sixteen people, a boat captain and three boats. This was early in January 1949. Ena packed my bag along with my flute and piccolo combination case and I left for Florida with Adrian. We took compartments on the train and arrived after a good rest. The weather was mild and soon I felt a lot better. Dixie prepared good meals and soon I was practicing flute and piccolo. Sometimes in the evening I would go down to their wine cellar and get a bottle of wine and have a couple of drinks before going to bed.

I was now feeling one hundred percent and would fish off Adrian's dock, which had a 200-foot walkway leading to it. I painted the railings in my spare time. The tropical fish were beautiful; you could see to the bottom in this clear blue water. At the end of ten days (I had been practicing flute and piccolo) I left for New York, feeling wonderful. I went back on "Stop the Music" and felt relaxed. The boys asked, "What happened to you, did the show get to you?"

I replied, "No, it was a combination of everything." I felt completely rejuvenated.

In October 1949 Ena saw a beautiful model home in the Roslyn Country Club section on Long Island. We had already built our summer home in a remote area in Shirley in 1947–8. We had no electric power there so we installed a power generator in the garage, which turned on automatically when a light switch was turned on. Three families on my road, including myself, had electricity and telephone wires strung for three miles from Montauk Highway.

We had a beautiful home in Roslyn Heights with a large living room, modern kitchen, three full bathrooms, four bedrooms and a den, which was opened by a bookcase door, where we had our TV set. On days off, when possible, we went out to our summer home where we lounged on the beautiful Westhampton beaches. We would usually eat at a place near the beach named the White Cap, where they served fish and chips.

The children had been taken out of parochial school when we moved and they were enrolled in public school in Roslyn

Heights, Adrienne moving to the seventh grade and little Arthur to the third grade. This little son of mine was a natural vocalist, singing beautifully at an early age. Today he is a fine singer and pianist and demands top dollar for his talents. I had a remarkably talented family.

I kept busy, having made a Disney soundtrack and a V-disc for Benny Goodman where he paid me well, also Musak recordings, record dates and transcriptions. We had done the "Philco" show in Boston on 1 July 1945 with great success. And I also worked with the vocalist Ginny Simms for several weeks while she was in town.

In April 1950 Tommy Dorsey called me from Texas and asked me to a Clambake Seven recording with him. He did not wish to transport his men from Texas. I knew Tommy well, having recorded with him as a sideman before he had his band. Tommy met us at the Victor recording studios. Peanuts Hucko was on clarinet, Bobby Hackett on trumpet, Buzzy Drootin on drums, Gene Schroeder on piano and Jack Lesberg on bass. Tommy, of course, was on trombone. It was a semi-dixieland group and we cut two sides, *Tiger Rag* and *Way down yonder in New Orleans*. We recorded the session late at night and were finished in about one and a half hours. I believe that this was one of Tommy Dorsey's last Clambake Seven recordings. Boomie Richman, his tenor man, received credit for the recording in *Down Beat*. When the magazine was distributed that month I showed it to Tommy Kay, our jazz guitarist. He said, "Who in hell is 'Boomie Richman'?"

I replied, "I don't know." I had never heard of him before, but was later to find out that he had become one of the finest tenor men in the country. He became a staff member of a small radio station in New York and I would listen to his cool sound and improvisations. I finally met Boomie one day at the Musical Instrument Exchange on 48th Street, where I bought my reeds and equipments, and we soon had a mutual admiration society going. He admired my Goodman recordings and I admired his great playing on the local radio station.

On 22 October 1952 the available Goodman boys, plus Helen Ward and Fletcher Henderson, gathered at the Columbia recording studio on 30th Street in New York to unveil the album

Treasure Chest of Performance Recordings, taken from air-checks from the Pennsylvania Hotel in 1937 and 1938.

It was during the early 1950s that Buddy Weed, his wife Sally, Ena and I went down to the George Washington Manor in Roslyn. Buddy sat down at the piano and started to play. He asked me to go home and get my horn. I did, and the first of a series of Wednesday night jam sessions was born. The following week others joined, and the sessions continued for about a year until Al Reiser, the bartender, left. Gilda Hermensen, an attractive red-head, and her husband Henry owned the place. A lot of drinks were given away and I doubt if the house made any money on these sessions, even though the place was crowded.

At ABC Whiteman booked a coming-out party for a debutante in the outskirts of a large midwestern city. He chartered a plane and made all preparations for the date. There were twenty-eight musicians, including three girl players. We were all immaculately dressed in tuxedos and the girls wore evening gowns. Whiteman had a little habit of going on a bender (getting drunk) about every three months for a couple days. This was one of those occasions.

We boarded the plane and flew to this city, where limousines were awaiting us. A truck and band boy were there to haul the instruments. We drove to the outskirts of the city, the truck following us, and we arrived at a beautiful mansion, surrounded by many acres of manicured lawn. By now Whiteman was half bombed. We entered the mansion and were greeted by the debutante's mother, a stately woman in her forties who carried a lorgnette, which she placed in front of her eyes when speaking to anyone. She told all of us to gather around her and placed the lorgnette in front of her eyes. I was standing next to Whiteman, who by now was feeling no pain. The woman addressed us and said, "Gentlemen, there are a few things that you can do for me. Please refrain from drinking. Another thing you can do, please refrain from smoking. Another thing that you can do for me, please sit at that table." It was a long table which would seat all of us. She went on and on. She continued, "One more thing that you can do for me, do not mingle with the guests." Whiteman started to twitch his feet impatiently as she repeated, "One more thing . . ."

Finally Whiteman impatiently said, "Madam, there is one small thing you can do for me."

She asked, "What is it Mr Whiteman?"

He replied without blinking an eye, "Go fuck yourself!"

She dropped her lorgnette and we all howled.

Whiteman was truly a great man with quick wit. But he was a gentle man. Some of the musicians were afraid of him, but I had no fear since I had worked for him way back in 1933 as a twenty-one-year-old boy. When he would bawl out the orchestra he would do so with tongue in cheek.

We soon went on a radio show that featured young instrumentalists and singers, where we had many talented performers. One day Whiteman came in to rehearsal and announced, "Well fellows, I'm sixty-seven years old today." He waited a few seconds for a reaction. I was next to him and exclaimed, "Paul, you don't look like sixty-seven." Actually, there wasn't a line on his face; he closely resembled Oliver Hardy of Laurel and Hardy fame, only with a little broader, thinner mustache. He said, "You don't believe me, I'll show you." He pulled his wallet out of his pocket and withdrew his driver's license and, as he did so, a $100 bill fell to the floor. He nonchalantly said, "Boys, do you believe me now?"

We were satisfied. It was obvious what the $100 bill was for. It was to pay off the police when he was arrested in one of his cars, his favorite being a German Porsche, which he often drove at high speeds when on a bender – but that was not often.

Three months elapsed and Whiteman went on another bender. He was picked up by a police car for doing eighty-two miles per hour in his Porche in New Jersey, where he now resided. The officer demanded his driver's license. Whiteman handed it to him. The officer opened it and saw the $100 bill. He asked Whiteman, "Is this yours?"

Whiteman promptly replied, "No it's yours!"

The officer said, "It's not mine," and proceeded to tear the bill into many pieces, which he threw on the ground. Then he gave Whiteman a speeding ticket. Paul told me about this confidentially and I hope that his wife Margaret, if she is alive, is not reading this book.

One night, after "The Teen Age Show," Paul asked us if we

wanted to hear Stan Kenton, who was playing nearby. I had known Stan slightly since the Goodman days when he was playing piano for Gil Evans on the West Coast. Whiteman, his assistant conductor Abe Osser, Lester Merkin (our first sax man), Maxie Cahn and I went to hear Kenton. Kenton spotted me. Whiteman's profile was facing him in the dimly lighted club. Suddenly Kenton stepped to the microphone and announced, "Ladies and gentlemen, we have a special guest in the house tonight." Whiteman began to unglue himself from his chair and was half-way to his feet. Kenton went on, "I would like to introduce Art Rollini, the fine tenor sax man formerly with the Benny Goodman band." The spotlight was on me and I took a bow. Whiteman sank down slowly in his chair. A half hour had elapsed before Kenton discovered Whiteman. He apologized profusely and Paul was introduced. He took a bow and sat down contentedly.

I played quite a few recording dates with Abe Osser. He was a mild-mannered man with great talent. The boys all liked him. We had other conductors, however. One was Ralph Wilkinson, a fine arranger who lived near me in Roslyn Heights; he had a sound-proof studio in his home where he would write sometimes all night. We would occasionally drive to work together. Ralph Hermann was another fine arranger and conductor. I did quite a few recordings with him, one of which was *Concerto for Doubles*, which he wrote for Al Gallodoro. He also wrote arrangements of Chopin's *Fantaisie-impromptu* and Jimmy Dorsey's *Oodles of Noodles*, which we recorded at Carnegie Hall with fifty men.

I was now in the ABC Symphony, playing third flute and piccolo. We had guest conductors each week: Sir Thomas Beecham, from England, was one. The conductors from all the large cities in the country were guests on Saturdays. It was a fine symphony orchestra, the woodwinds consisting mostly of doublers, except for Victor Just, a fine flutist and Barrère student. Joe Small, who doubled alto sax, clarinet and baritone sax, played second flute. He was self-taught. Al Gallodoro played first clarinet with ease. He never used an A clarinet, for he could transpose almost anything at sight. We had a legitimate oboe player, Harry Schulman, and Lenny Portnoy on second oboe, a doubler who could play anything from a baritone sax to a Jew's harp. Irving Horowitz, the english horn player, had an exceptionally fine sound. Herman Yorks excelled on first bassoon and Lester Merkin, our alto sax man, played second bassoon.

George Gaber was our first drummer, and an excellent timpanist who could play jazz drums almost as well. Dick Ridgely, our second drummer, played fine xylophone, vibes and chimes. The brass consisted mostly of good dance men, except for Alfred Corrado on french horn, who played with a strong tone. Charlie Small (sometimes Jack Elliot) was on first trombone and Vernon Brown on second. Phil Cadway was fine on tuba. Gloria Agostino was our harpist, and unbelievably great.

I can't go through the names of all these great artists, but Arnold Eidus, who played a Stradivarius, was on first violin, backed up by Leo Kahn, Maxie Cahn and Anthony Di Girolamo; George Ricci was a superb cellist. Frank Vagnoni had one of the best symphony orchestras in the country.

Dick Ridgely, who became a close friend, told me an amusing story one day. He told me about an incident that happened years before, when he played a club date in New Jersey. He was on his way back to New York City from his date, when he was picked up by a police patrol car for speeding just before reaching the Holland Tunnel. The officer asked to see his driver's license and registration. Dick told him that he was very tired and wanted to get home as soon as possible. He pleaded with the officer, "Please let me go, I am tired and want to go home. I'll give you everything I have in my wallet, which is not much, but please let me go."

The officer said, "OK." Dick opened his wallet and all he had was two dollars. The officer accepted this. As the policeman was about to leave, Dick called to him. He said desperately, "Officer, I have to go through the Holland Tunnel and I don't have the fifty cents toll." The officer reached into his pocket and promptly gave him fifty cents back.

Dick had an extremely high voice and, when I would call him on the phone, I would not recognize his voice and would invariably ask, "May I speak to your father?" I thought that it was one of his children answering the phone. He would say in his high-pitched voice, "This is Dick speaking."

While at ABC Dick went to bigger and better things. He bought a home in Smithtown, Long Island, and purchased many acres of property there. Together with a builder he built a development of many homes. He finished this project, and was looking for something bigger. He finally found it. One day at ABC he came to me and asked if I would become his partner in a small steak house in Watermill, Long Island, called the Trade Winds. I rejected the deal because it was too far from ABC and the travel would have been too much. So Dick opened by himself and featured first Tommy Furtado, a handsome young man who had sung on the ABC Saturday night "Dancing Party," on piano and vocals. Dick often invited our jazz group for steaks and drinks. We had a good time playing there.

Meanwhile, back at ABC, we had another conductor who arranged well and who would often give me solos. His name was Al Datz. Hank D'Amico was still on staff playing third alto and jazz clarinet, and Peanuts Hucko was now playing good jazz clarinet and tenor, although he seldom had the chance to be heard solo. I taped one jazz show that he played with Hank D'Amico leading, and he played a magnificent tenor solo on *Strike up the Band*. Hank was original; he played clarinet with a unique style. Peanuts had a fine ear, but was influenced by Benny Goodman on clarinet and Eddie Miller on tenor sax. We had another tenor man on staff, who arranged brilliantly. His name was Nick Caiazza. He often covered for me when Ena was hospitalized. He very seldom got the chance to write, though he did do some arrangements for Billy Butterfield, who had a segment on "Dancing Party."

"Dancing Party" was a radio program that ran for three hours on Saturday nights and featured many types of music. There was Maurice Pierre, a society group, Ralph Hermann, featuring the Hal Kemp style, and Abe Osser with a large group including strings, which played pop music. Al Datz had a dance orchestra, which also played pop music (without strings), and Billy Butterfield had a segment featuring jazz in big-band form, mainly with Gil Evans and Nick Caiazza charts. I also had a couple shots with my own jazz group consisting of six men.

Osser had a good orchestra on "Dancing Party." Tony Faso played first trumpet, and the rest of the trumpet section consisted of the Morreale brothers, Jim and Jack, Bobby Hackett, a star in his own right, and Johnny Fallstich, who would invariably play the lead on ballads. On trombones were Charlie Small, Vernon Brown, Kai Winding (for a while) and others, including Jack Elliot. The saxes consisted of Lester Merkin, Joe Small, Hank D'Amico or Peanuts Hucko, Lenny Portnoy and myself. The personnel on this program was not always the same, but the rhythm section usually consisted of Dave Bowman on piano, Tommy Kay on guitar, Felix Giobbe on bass and Morey Feld on drums. All in all, it was an excellent staff.

At the ABC studios we played the Metropolitan Opera auditions for thirteen weeks each year. The winner would go to sing at the Met. These shows were conducted by Fausto Cleva, a fine conductor, but a tyrant.

Often, on other shows with smaller orchestras, I would play first flute, and found myself able to taper off on high F♯ and G♯, down to a whisper. I felt comfortable now, long since playing my Powell flute and piccolo. This sense of elation did not last for long, however. Gradually, in the middle of 1955, I found my flute embouchure (lip) deteriorating. (The other instruments were OK, however.) As time went on it became worse, and soon I was struggling. After a show one day I asked Victor Just (our first flute player) to help me. We went to a small empty studio. He could do nothing. I now panicked. I took a couple of lessons from Harold Bennett of the Met. No avail. I went to Jimmy Politas, who shared the first chair at the Met with Bennett, and took several lessons from him. No avail. I then went back to Henry Zlotnick, my original teacher, but he could not help me either.

All of those years of study had gone for naught. I was desperate because Vagnoni depended on my flute double. He saw that I was in trouble when I handed my flute parts to other doublers, but he said nothing.

I called our family physician, Larry Kryle, in Roslyn Heights and visited him in sheer desperation. He had saved Ena's life several times and now I sought his help. He said to me, "Art, I am going to send you to a psychiatrist." I wound up with Dr Anchel of Garden City. He interviewed me and gave me a series of shock treatments. That did not help. He sent me back to Larry Kryle. Every day was like a nightmare and every night I couldn't sleep.

Larry suggested that I go on a cruise alone and so I booked passage on the S.S. *Nassau*, which was to sail to Nassau in the Bahamas. Ena manicured my nails and packed my bags knowing that there were five women to every man on board. I called Vagnoni and asked for a leave of absence. One Friday evening Ena drove me to New York and I boarded the ship, without my flute, bid Ena goodbye and we steamed away.

The first thing I did was go to the purser's desk to check my valuables and money. He looked up to me and said, "We have another Rollini on board."

"Impossible," I thought. I had looked in every telephone directory in all of the then forty-eight states. I asked him, "Where?"

He said, "Marcel Rollini, the chief radio operator."

"How can I get to see him?" I asked excitedly.

He said, "Go far up to the top of the ship and you will find his apartment."

Now this ship had an Italian crew, many of whom could speak no English. I knocked on Marcel's door and he opened it. He was a good-looking man, about fifty years old, with receding hair, and very handsome in his uniform. I introduced myself and he almost dragged me into his apartment. He spoke little English but we were able to communicate. It seems that we were related through our grandfathers. We chatted until the ship was far out to sea. He asked, "Do you want to call your wife?"

I replied eagerly, "Yes." In a minute I was speaking to Ena. We exchanged greetings and then she asked, "How do you feel?"

I said, "Fine, as long as I am away from that damn flute."

I had a wonderful week. The food was excellent, I went swimming and skeet-shooting, and played shuffle-board, ping-pong and cards. I even danced with some of the girls. Soon I had completely forgotten about my problems.

On the return voyage I was beginning to feel a little concerned about returning to my problem. At the ship's ball I wore my white dinner jacket and danced with several girls—secretaries, models, doctors' wives, nurses—no help! Ena was waiting for me when I arrived at the pier. She looked pretty and sped me home to Roslyn Heights. The first thing I did was to go into our den and try my flute. No good!

I went back to work on Monday at ABC. The sax and clarinet were fine, but not the flute. Whenever I knew that there were difficult flute parts on a show I would send in a substitute, having checked at the music library. I struggled for three whole years, going on two more cruises—the same routine!

Then Ray McKinley, my old friend, came in to do a two-hour daily television show called "That's Entertainment." He asked for me. On this show, which started rehearsal at 10 a.m., I passed my flute parts to another man, usually Lester Merkin, sometimes Lenny Portnoy, sometimes Nick Caiazza—anybody. I was content to play the tenor background for our vocalist. We would go on the air at noon and finish at 2 p.m.; then came rehearsal, until 4 p.m., for the next day. Tom Poston, a fine comedian, and "Professor" Irwin Corey were on this show. The latter was zany, coming out with a rumpled full dress suit, sneakers and string tie. He broke us up every day.

This show ran for six months. I drank very little at this time. On the last day, a Friday, however, I bought a pint of vodka, and after the show I had a drink to celebrate. There was no rehearsal in the afternoon because this was the end. I put the bottle in its paper bag and put it in my sax case. Vagnoni had something special for me that afternoon. I got back to the main studio and found myself the only flute in the orchestra. It was a longhair show. I looked at the music and shuddered. Al Gallodoro was playing clarinet next to me on my left. Vagnoni was sitting in the control room. I struggled: my flute lip was shot. After the show Al Gallodoro turned to me and said, "Nice work, Art."

I exclaimed, "Are you kidding?" I opened my sax case to put my flute away. Frank Vagnoni came over to me and demanded, "What's in the bag?" I explained the situation to him. He said, "See me in my office." On the way I put my case in my locker and went into his office. He said, "Sit down." I did so. Then he continued, "Will you substitute for Herman Yorks tomorrow at 1 o'clock? He has to go somewhere." I readily accepted and breathed a sigh of relief. That is the way Frank was.

We did a large orchestra rock program with Merv Griffin on radio on Friday nights. "Dancing Party" was about to go off the air after, I believe, five years. "The Merv Griffin Show" did not last too long (the ratings were low) and "Dancing Party" went off.

There was nothing left. Some programs moved to the West Coast and came contract time. Most of us would go to the office and pick up our checks on Wednesday. We did not work. I was embarrassed and would walk into the office backwards. On alternate Wednesdays Brownie or Johnny Fallstich would pick up the checks. Then ABC demanded a cut in the sixty-five man staff.

On Monday 6 October 1958 the "Breakfast Club" came to town from Chicago for a week. Eddie Ballantine, the leader, asked for me to play flute and Vagnoni was sitting in the front row. I declined. I handed the parts to Nick Caiazza and I played his clarinet parts. The following Saturday I received my eight weeks notice from Vagnoni. I was elated because finally I was free. In his formal notice Vagnoni asked me to see him in his office on my day of departure. I did so and the first thing he asked me was, "How's your flute lip?"

I nodded my head sadly and said, "No good Frank." We shook hands and he promised to call me again.

I did the Sid Caesar rehearsal for the last "Show of Shows" in Brooklyn on December 6th. The next night, at the same place, I bumped into Phil Claro and Eleanor Bishop, dear friends of mine, who were visiting one of the personnel on the show. Tony Scott was a guest and we waved greetings. On December 23rd I did a TV commercial with Buddy Weed, and played that night at Brookville Country Club with Felix Giobbe. Frank Vagnoni called me for "The Patti Page Show," which consisted of a rehearsal on the 27th and the show on the 28th. I worked New Years' Eve with Giobbe at the Brookville Country Club. For all intents and purposes this was the end of the "thirty years." I knew that, without my flute double, I was through with commercial radio and TV.

EIGHT

Epilogue

Early in January 1959 I visited Paul Small, brother of Joe, Charlie and Hy. He had built a laundromat in College Point, Queens, and I was very interested. I called Bob Suling, an ALD representative for Westinghouse, and he showed me a good location to build a store in Roslyn. It had formerly been a five and ten cent store and was now defunct. We signed the lease for the store at the end of the month.

I was not busy in music, nor did I look for work, but on January 18th I did an Italian variety show at Carnegie Hall. My old friend Irving Brodsky, originally with the California Ramblers, was playing piano. It was nice to see him after so many years. A week later I did a club date and two shows, and on February 7th worked at Wheatly Country Club with Giobbe.

On April 8th Ena and I went down to celebrate Benny Goodman's 25th anniversary on the forming of his band. This was held at the 21 Club in New York. Hymie Shertzer and his wife Addie went too; he and I were the only original men there, Red Ballard being out on the West Coast. Helen Ward and Peggy Lee were also present.

Ena and I formed a corporation for the laundromat. I asked her, "What should we call it?" With her quick mind, she promptly replied, "Artena Laundromat, Inc." We had a send-off party, and opened the store at 8 a.m. on 25th May. We had sent out 5000 flyers through an advertising agency offering one free machine-load of wash per customer. The place was jammed. Westinghouse, free of charge, sent an attractive girl in a white uniform to demonstrate how to use the machines. Customers used up to ten machines apiece. Everything went wrong. The dryers were supposed to be wired individually; instead, they had two on a line. Some of the washing-machine hoses burst because of the water pressure being too great. I called my service men and they kept changing hoses. The place was bedlam. By 6 p.m. we had done 350 washes. We went on until eleven o'clock that night and at ten I locked the door and would only let people out, not in.

The next day I had the electricians in early and, one by one, they wired the dryers individually. I got a water-pressure reducer installed and everything was now in order. We went on and on. Even though the parking was inadequate, we had the only laundromat for miles around and continued to do well. Our place was attended at all times; the others weren't.

One day Mike Krasnopolski, the fine concert bassist from the NBC orchestra, came in. He had had trouble with his washing machine and this was an emergency. While his clothes were washing he told me a couple stories about Leopold Spitalny the concert conductor, who had been with NBC before Arturo Toscanini. On one occasion Spitalny was conducting Tchaikovsky's *Nutcracker Suite* at rehearsal and the orchestra sounded badly. Spitalny said, in his heavy accent, "If Tchaikovsky vas alive, he'd toin over in his grave!" Another time, during a rehearsal, one of the men stopped the orchestra and said, "Mr Spitalny, I have a wrong note on my sheet." Spitalny promptly answered, "Put a cross around it!"

Different musicians would drop in. Teddy Kotsoftis and Felix Giobbe, both bass players, came in and we always had a laugh. Teddy told me a story about Lester Lanin. At this time Lanin was quite busy doing dates in Washington, DC. One day when he was in his office working the phone rang and his secretary answered it. She said, "Mr Lanin, it's the White House."

He said, without blinking an eye, "Ask them if it is important."

There was a story floating around about Phil Napoleon, the fine dixieland trumpet player. It seems that he had a club date at a hospital for the mentally disturbed on Ward's Island, which is located beneath the Queensboro bridge in New York City. He took the elevator down to the island and entered the hospital. Somehow he got lost in the corridors and was wandering around. A man with a white coat appeared and Phil asked directions. The man inquired, "What's your name?"

Phil said, "Napoleon." The man grabbed him roughly by the arm and said, "Come with me!"

Ena found it more and more difficult to come down to the store, the invisible lint bothering her lungs. She would send hot meals down when she couldn't be there. I was tired, but at least I didn't have to worry about the flute any longer. Business was good, almost too good, because I didn't have enough machines for the demand and I had no room to install more.

Ena and I sold the house. We needed it no longer, as Adrienne was married, and Arthur had joined the voluntary draft at the age of 18, when he finished high school. We moved to an apartment on Main Street, Roslyn, and could see the Hempstead Bay from our living room window.

One day I answered the phone and who was it but Benny Goodman. As I picked up the phone, I answered, "Roslyn Laundromat."

Benny chuckled and said, "Schneeze, are you in the laundry business now?"

I replied, "Sort of." He continued, "I am going into Freedom Land in the Bronx. Do you want to go?" After he mentioned a price, which was far below what I was earning, I declined, saying that I couldn't get away. He then asked, "Do you know a good piano player?" I suggested Mickey Crane (Carrano). He asked me about a good first alto man, and I mentioned a couple of men.

Time went on at the laundromat. We were very busy, but I felt boxed in. Ena would come in briefly to relieve me so that I could go to the apartment half a mile away to rest. Invariably Mrs Stein, who lived directly below us, would start to play her Hammond organ just as I lay down. This organ boomed loudly and Mrs Stein would often skip beats, which disturbed me greatly. I never could rest when I came home, but I never complained to the Steins and often took a nap in our car instead.

Business was booming, but that wasn't to last. Five other stores were under construction within a five-mile radius. As they opened one by one the business began to slide. I called a business broker and he guaranteed me a sale in one month. But I did not like his price, nor the fact that there was only to be a small down-payment and the rest on three-year large notes, so I declined.

I worked at Wheatley Country Club on Saturday nights with Felix Giobbe, always the band clown. He had a natural wit and would make me laugh just to look at him. We would compare noses and laugh.

Felix had a good quartet at the Wheatley Country Club: Mickey Crane on piano, Morey Feld on drums, Felix on bass and myself on tenor. We would do nothing outside of playing but laugh.

Felix was commissioned to paint a mural in the Roslyn Savings Bank. The bank gave him the keys to work on Sundays. One Sunday, while taking a breather, he accidentally stepped on the burglar alarm. The place was soon swarming with squad cars. He was embarrassed! Felix went on to paint more bank murals after this. On one bank job he was painting on his scaffold when there was a hold-up. He went on painting as if nothing was happening. Felix continued playing during these years. His bass sounded beautiful, especially when he played with a bow; he had the vibrato of a fine cellist.

At the laundromat, business was still sliding. I thought I had sold it when a buyer gave me a large deposit check, subject to examination of the books. He came in the following day and I gave him the books to study; he went to the back room for two hours. Even these books showed a decline. He demanded his check back and I was totally disheartened.

I stared out the window and looked longingly at the people playing tennis in the courts across the street. I saw people passing by in their bathing suits. I felt truly boxed in. But business was really not that bad, and we lived well: we had two cars plus a summer home. It would have been adequate for most people.

Ena's doctor bills contributed to our expenses; in the last year at the laundromat she was hospitalized three times. I decided to unload at any price. I was desperate. Two gentlemen came in and made me a ridiculously low offer. I said to them, "Come back in half an hour while I think it over." They left and I pondered. When they came back I told them that I would accept.

Ena was still weak when we closed shop on 5 August 1965. We still had a month to go on our apartment lease, but we packed our clothes and headed for our summer home in Shirley, Long Island. I felt free again. We loafed a month in Shirley and went back to the apartment to move. Vince Teolis, our son-in-law, had rented a U-haul truck, and he and his friend Frank Rada helped us move. The men had already started cleaning the stove and other things in the apartment which were sorely neglected when Ena was hospitalized so often. We headed back to Shirley and loafed some more. After several months I looked at our bank balance and saw it dwindling. I placed an ad in the *Long Island Advance* for teaching music. The ad read, "Now available for teaching sax and clarinet: Art Rollini, formerly with Benny Goodman, Paul Whiteman and the ABC musical staff." I received just one call from that ad, but it was a rather important one. It was from Pete Mezzapella, a local bandleader who had multiple jobs on the weekends. He asked me to come down to Mastic Beach nearby to see him. I did, and he started to book me on his extra jobs as leader. The bookings were slow at first but then they became more numerous. I was working with others then too, including Joe Caffi.

I stayed at the Country Flower Shop with Dick Benedix for six months. I had been working for him five days a week and decided I wanted a change for the better. Meanwhile I went down to Patchogue Floral Fantasyland in Patchogue and applied for a job with Hans Von Ginhoven, the owner. I started immediately. The job did not pay much more per day, but I was to work six days per week and I still had Saturday nights and Sundays off for music. I worked in Riverhead with Pete's big band, which was fronted by Johnny Bruno, a fine jazz accordion player. Pete was content to sit and play guitar, although he also played bass. We had a top-notch band of top players and the charts were good. I enjoyed it.

Somehow Jack Ellsworth, the disc jockey and manager of radio station WALK in Patchogue, found out that I was in Shirley and began to give me plugs on the air whenever the Goodman records were played. I wrote to him and he responded by inviting me to the studios.

Early in January 1968 I received an invitation from Benny Goodman to attend the 30th-year reunion of the Carnegie Hall concert. I called his secretary and accepted. On January 16th, the day of the reunion, Ena was in the hospital again, but I went anyway, picking up Vernon Brown on the way in at Roslyn Heights. We proceeded to the penthouse, where the party was to take place.

There were many people there—reporters, and most of my old buddies, including Hymie Shertzer and his lovely wife Addie, Helen and Chris Griffin, George Koenig, Jess Stacey, Ziggy Elman and Martha Tilton, the last three flown in from the West Coast by Benny. Helen Ward was there. I kissed all the girls and shook hands with all the men, including Gene Krupa. Gene hadn't changed a bit—still the clean-cut handsome man that I had known many years earlier.

In walked Benny, well tanned and wearing a light blue suit. He had just returned from the Caribbean and I was the first to greet him. I gave him a bear hug and pressed against his unshaven cheek. He said, "Hello, Schneeze," and gently nudged me aside to get to the others. It had been a long time indeed. I hadn't seen Benny since 8 April 1959, when he had invited us to the 21 Club in New York to celebrate the 25th anniversary of the formation of his band.

I was followed by a group of reporters and did not have time to get my first drink. They asked me to go on a taped interview with William B. William of WNEW. I said, "Sure." I was seated at a table with Martha Tilton, Ziggy Elman, George Koenig, Gene Krupa and Jess Stacy. William asked me what I thought of rock. I could think of nothing but to echo Benny's sentiments which he had expressed on a late TV show a short time before. Benny sat down and Gene Krupa introduced these guests at the table for the taped interview. I believe he introduced Martha first, then Ziggy, and finally when he came to me he said, "And here is Schneeze Rollini."

William asked, "Why do you call him Schneeze?"

Benny piped up, "Because he has a big nose!" Tactless Benny, I thought "the best jazz clarinet player in the world!"

Fortunately that part of the tape was deleted.

We ate and drank and were hounded by reporters. They all asked me what I was doing at the time. I told one that I was in the wholesale flower business. Another from *Newsday* that I was in the flower business.

He asked me, "How's business?"

I answered, "OK."

We posed for the centerfold of *Esquire* magazine and the party went on with drinks and food. Even the great Urbie Green was there and feeling no pain by now. We, by now, were all feeling good. I kissed Martha Tilton, Helen Ward, Helen Griffin and Addie Shertzer. They all asked about Ena, who had been such a good friend. They were sorry indeed to learn that she was in the hospital, and they all asked me to say hello to her.

I did not go to work the next day, but the following day the boys, with Neil, Matty, Lucas, Fred and the rest, had the *Newsday* article tacked to the huge post. It quoted me as saying that I was in the flour business! We all laughed.

I stayed at Patchogue Floral for seven months with Hans, doing club dates weekends. Then Vince Teolis, my son-in-law, who worked as batcher for Certified Industries in their plant at Ronkonkoma, told me that there was an opening for a state concrete inspector's job. I called Jerry Murphy, the manager of the Long Island office, and he asked me to see him the following morning. He told me that the job was mine. I bid adieu to Hans, Fred, the man who took orders on the telephone, and the little British secretary who often made me a cup of strong tea at the coffee break. (She would put a potfull serving into one cup, so that it would appear almost like the color of coffee.) The next morning I drove to Franklin Square in Nassau County and met Jerry Murphy. Jerry was a congenial man and so was Jack Martin, his assistant—a Goodman fan. I filled out the necessary papers and they assigned me to a plant for training.

So I spent the next five years with the Pittsburgh Testing Lab. Then in March 1973 we lost the state contract due to an austerity budget program in Albany, and we had to train state men to take our places. I called Cosimo (Cee) Morabito of Municipal Testing Laboratory in Hicksville. I knew of him as an ex-drummer and he knew of me. He hired me on the spot. After filling in the necessary papers Cee put me right to work.

All these years I had been playing music weekends, and teaching some nights. Ena had been in the hospital several times during this span, and on 22 December 1977 she passed away. She had been hospitalized for 117 days in 1977. With an advanced stage of emphysema, her heart finally gave out. Cee and Jay at the Lab sent the most beautiful floral arrangement that I had ever seen. Ena was buried in Kensico cemetery in our family plot on a hill overlooking a pond in Valhalla, New York.

It was the last week in April 1978 that my son, Arthur Jr, came up from Florida, where he had played a trio engagement for seven and a half months with a fine drummer and Jerry Jerome on tenor. He arrived in his new Chevy soft-top truck crammed full of equipment, including a smart racing bicycle standing in the extreme rear end for his daily exercise. He set up his equipment in our small living room, taking up about one third of its area. The equipment consisted of a Fender–Rhodes piano with bass reflex (which he had had installed), two amps, a mike with boom and a sideman Rhythm Ace with a stop pedal for pick-ups, and a tuning device which he used daily to tune his piano. He sang and played magnificently. He knows some five hundred songs and I believe that he is one of the best singles in the country. I asked, "Are you still playing jazz, son?"

He replied "No, Dad, I have played black jazz spots throughout the South and only saved enough to buy myself a ham sandwich."

On April 30th young Arthur was guest on "The Sunday Brunch," and I invited the Don Colgan group from the Better 'Ole to come over after their job. I invited Sonny Dallas, the great bassist with the Lennie Tristano group for many years who is now a professor of music at Suffolk Community College, Long Island. Soon the little house was rocking with some of the greatest jazz my son and I had ever heard. Sonny Dallas had to leave and we continued with young Gary Hoff on upright bass. This young man has unusual technique for a bassist.

Our beautiful Sunday session was soon over. Young Art and I played the tape we made of it over and over after the boys had left. I helped my son load his truck with all his equipment and bicycle and, after a brief night's rest, we awakened at 4:15 a.m. Young Art wanted to beat the traffic into and through New York City, as he was off to an engagement at the O'Hare-American Inn in Des Plaines, Illinois, a suburb of Chicago. I had to leave in a little while for my day job.

On May 2nd I left the house at five o'clock in the morning to go to work in a plant called Advanced in West Babylon, Long Island, owned by Sandy Nicolia. When my neighbor John Costadura was leaving for work a couple of hours later he noticed smoke coming out of my chimney and roof vents. He immediately called our neighbor John Savoca, who was a volunteer fireman for the Ridge Fire Department, but by the time the firemen got there the house was ablaze. My neighbor fought the fire.

Word reached me at Advanced at 9 a.m. that the house had been destroyed. I continued on to my next assignment at Carlson & Sons, a precast concrete plant in King's Park, Long Island, where I had a little shipping to do. I had the radio on in the car and heard reports of numerous brush fires in Suffolk County. I lived in a wooded area and assumed that this was the cause of the fire, because it had not rained in twelve days.

All the way home I continued to hear reports of brush fires and still thought that that was the cause of the fire. I reached home at noon and found my home completely gutted. I put my daily report in the mail box, flag up, and entered my little home. Everything had been destroyed: clothing, band pictures, scrapbook, tapes, stereo tape recorder, TV set, "Hall of Fame" certificate for Benny Goodman's Carnegie Hall Concert 1950 release, microphones, amplifiers, all of Ena's clothing, stationery, etc. My office floor was burned out, the telephone disintegrated. My instruments, tenor sax and clarinet, were still standing, completely burned out. My mouthpieces had melted. My conductor's stand had disintegrated. Air conditioner, thermostats, everything was lost, including the beautiful tape that had been recorded less than two full days before. There was a gaping hole in the roof. The carpeting had all gone.

Fortunately I had paid most of my bills before May 1st, so had no immediate problem there. I looked at where my desk had been and the wall there was mostly charred. There was the culprit: a burned out electrical outlet. I had noticed a flickering of my desk lamp for two days and, thinking that it was a bad socket in the lamp, I had kept it off as much as possible. I moved in with my daughter Adrienne in Bay Shore that night with nothing but the clothes on my back.

I spent two weeks with Adrienne, buying a few things and going to my burned out home daily for the mail, a distance of about twenty-four miles each way. Finally, through the insurance company, a furnished trailer was set up on my property and I took my smoke-sodden suits to the London Dry Cleaners in Shirley.

They tried, but to no avail, to save my clothes after several cleanings.

The builders arrived, headed by John Seeger of the Apple Construction Company representing the Brite Builders, who deal in fires only. John was a bright young man of about thirty years, a musical talent, who had recorded a radio commercial. John sings and plays guitar, and his tape, which he played for me, featured sound on sound, bass and keyboard. Some of his men were equally talented playing guitar. One of the men had an uncle by the name of Vido Musso, of Benny Goodman and Stan Kenton fame. We chatted about Vido while they worked. My neighbor John Savoca, who gallantly fought the flames in my home, installed the carpeting. Another neighbor, Pat Licavoli, a floor man, installed the tiles in my kitchen and bath, and I was comfortable in my little home again.

4 May 1982 was declared Benny Goodman Birthday Month on Radio Station WLIM in Patchogue, and Goodman music was played from dawn to dusk. I visited the studios, only a short distance from home, and saw Benny for the first time since the 30th year reunion of the Carnegie Hall Jazz Concert. Benny and I had a nice chat and we were both interviewed on the air. I asked Benny if he would like to come to my home, only ten minutes away, but he declined, saying that he had to get home to practice.

To this day I think that Benny Goodman was still the greatest all-around clarinet player. Although he did not keep pace with today's progressive chord changes, and relied on nostalgia for the most part, he was a creator and influenced many players of his instrument throughout the world. I'll have to give the number two spot to Artie Shaw, who was so great. The rest are up for grabs: Johnny Mince, Tony Scott, Peanuts Hucko, Barney Bigard, Pete Fountain, Abe Most, Buddy DeFranco, Gus Bivona, Hank D'Amico, Phil Bodner, Walter Levinsky, Mahlon Clark, Matty Matlock, Joe Dixon, Woody Herman, Clarence Hutchenrider, Sol Yaged, Bob Wilber, Buster Bailey, Marshall Royal, Joe Viola, Artie Baker, Paul Ricci, Tony Parenti, Jimmy Lytell, Sal Pace, Pete Pumiglio, Sal Franzella, Drew Page, Izzy Friedman and newcomer Dick Johnson—other names slip my mind at the moment. I must apologize for this. Of course, all of these men are in the American field, but there are many great foreigners, too. In my estimation, my friend Al Gallodoro is the best technician in the world, followed by a close second, Vincent "Jimmy" Abato. Both are excellent players, who double alto saxophone and bass clarinet as well.

In 1978 I met a wonderful woman, Elizabeth Buley, who has been my constant companion. We were married on 15 September 1984 and moved to Florida early in 1985.

I must close now.

Musically yours,

Art Rollini

Index